family field guide

— S E R I E S —

VOLUME ONE

Rocky Mountain Mammals

written by
Garrick Pfaffmann

illustrated by
Hilary Forsyth

BearBop Press LLC

BASALT COLORADO USA

field notes

field notes

ISBN-13: 978-1-882426-24-9

ISBN-10: 1-882426-24-X

Published by:

BearBop Press, LLC

Illustrated by:

Hilary Forsyth

Designed by:

words pictures colours graphic design

Distributed by:

WHO Press

www.whopress.com

Library of Congress Control Number: 200692310

Author's Dedication

To people of all ages
with curiousity and wonder in tact;
and to young people,
who remind us old people,
lest we forget.

Illustrator's Dedication

For all who have an eye for
beauty in nature's creativity.
Art, color and design,
let all forms of creation
come to life.

ACKNOWLEDGEMENTS

Thanks to Warren Ohlrich of Who Press for guiding and advising us through the publishing process. Thanks to Kelly Alford of words pictures colours graphic design for turning our drawings and text into an enticing product. Thanks to the Aspen Center for Environmental Studies (ACES) and Cabela's for sharing their animal mounts. Thanks to Janis Huggins and Warren and Karen Ohlrich for editing and shaping the final pages. Thanks to John and Lindsay for listening to us talk so, so, so much about this project and for supporting our ridiculous dedication along the way. Thanks to Mason for waiting just long enough to enter this world, so that this book could be completed on time.

How To Use This Book

FIND THE FOLLOWING INFORMATION ON EACH MAMMAL PAGE
Animal name
Animal habitat (food, shelter, water and range)
Common predators or prey
Animal birth cycles and litter sizes
Animal interactions with humans
Interesting facts

THESE PAGES AND CHAPTERS SUPPORT INFORMATION FOUND ON EACH MAMMAL PAGE

Symbols (p. 10) Use the symbols on each animal page to learn the most basic information about where the animal lives, what time of day it is most active, what it eats, its role in the food chain and how it survives winter.

Where They Live (p. 12) This chapter supports the first symbol on each page (where the animal lives) by providing an illustration of what to expect in each *life zone* in summer and in winter, photographs of plants that help identify each life zone and interesting facts about each life zone.

Appendix (p. 86) Information in the appendix is organized to support the other symbols (what they eat, where they live, when are they most active, their role in the food chain and winter survival strategies) and to easily compare animals' behaviors.

Glossary (p.96) Hard-to-understand words are written in italics. Definitions for these words are organized in alphabetical order in the glossary.

Index (p. 100) Select a topic from the index, locate the page listed next to the topic to find the needed information.

INDEPENDENDENT READING LEVELS

First Grade Use the photographs, illustrations and symbols to learn basic body parts, where the animal lives, what time of day it is most active, what it eats and how it survives winter.

Second Grade Use the photographs, illustrations, symbols, habitat information and short snippets of interesting facts about each animal.

Third-Eighth Grades Paragraphs of interesting background are written in language and text size appropriate for young readers. All elements of a non-fiction book and field guide are present including table of contents, glossary, background knowledge of ecosystems and references for further reading.

family field guide

Contents

Being A Naturalist

WHAT IS A NATURALIST?

A naturalist is a person who observes nature and tries to understand how things in nature (plants, animals, weather, rocks, soil) work with each other.

Some naturalists are young, some are old and some are right in the middle. Some naturalists live in the country, some in the city and some in the suburbs. Some naturalists like mountains, others deserts, rivers, oceans or gardens. Some naturalists are rich as kings, others have hardly a home. Some naturalists read books to understand more, others just like to watch. Some naturalists draw pictures, write words, build forts and play hide-and-seek. A naturalist is any person, no matter their age, who explores the natural environment and takes time to think about how nature works and how people work as a part of nature.

NATURALIST TOOLS

Eyes

Ears

Nose

Fingers

Brain

To see, hear, smell, touch and think about the surroundings.

Binoculars

Hand-lenses

Cameras

Paints and brushes

Pencils and sketchbooks

Notepads and pens

To look and see more carefully!

family field guide

NATURALIST RULES

SAFETY FIRST

Explore with a friend.

Tell others where you are going.

Bring water, sunscreen, a snack, a hat and a rainjacket.

Pay attention to where you are and what is around you.

RESPECT WILDLIFE

Watch animals from a safe distance so not to disturb them.

Never chase or tease animals.

Never feed wild animals.

LEAVE NO TRACE

Stay on the path when using trails.

Take all garbage home with you.

Walk quietly so others are not disturbed.

TIPS FOR SUCCESS

Explore at dawn and dusk.

Leave pets at home.

Sit in one place for a while so animals come find you.

Think strategically: where do they feed, drink, sleep, rest?

Look in all directions: up, down, side to side.

FAMOUS NATURALISTS

ANSEL ADAMS (1902-1984) Photographer; helped people see the beauty of natural landscapes.

DAVID BROWER (1912-2000) Longtime president of the Sierra Club, soldier, activist and lover of wild places.

RACHEL CARSON (1907-1964) Biologist, ecologist and author who wrote the book *Silent Spring* which helped stop the use of chemicals in farming.

ENOS MILLS (1870-1922) Author and naturalist who helped create Rocky Mountain National Park near Estes Park, Colorado.

JOHN MUIR (1838-1914) Author and naturalist who helped protect and create Yosemite National Park in California.

HENRY DAVID THOREAU (1817-1862) Author and naturalist who lived at Walden Pond in Massachusetts.

THEODORE ROOSEVELT (1858-1919) President of the United States from 1905-1909. Created the first forest preserves.

Symbols

The following symbols are used throughout the book. Symbols are located on each animal page. Look at the symbols on the animal page, then read these explanations to understand what they mean.

WHERE Where the animal lives and seasonal patterns.

 LOWLAND SHRUB AND FOREST
see page 12 for more information

 MONTANE FOREST
see page 12 for more information

 SUBALPINE FOREST
see page 13 for more information

 ALPINE TUNDRA
see page 13 for more information

 RIPARIAN ECOSYSTEM
see page 13 for more information

WHEN When the animal is most active.

 DIURNAL
active in daytime, sleeps at night

 NOCTURNAL
active at night, sleeps all day

 CREPUSCULAR
active mostly at dawn and dusk

family field guide

WINTER How the animal survives cold temperatures, deep snow and limited food.

MIGRATE
moves to lower elevations and sunny slopes

HIBERNATE
"sleeps" through winter; heart rate and breathing slow, body temperature cools

ADAPT
survives comfortably in the cold and snow

TOLERATE
has long periods of rest and sleep, but continues to feed regularly

FOOD What types of food the animal prefers.

HERBIVORE
mostly plants

OMNIVORE
both plants and other animals

CARNIVORE
mostly other animals

ROLE The animal's main role in the food chain.

PREDATOR
eats other animals

PREY
eaten by other animals

SCAVENGER
eats garbage and dead animals (carrion)

Where They Live

Animals, like people, can only live in places where they can find the right food, the right temperatures, the right materials for shelter and plenty of water. In the mountains, food, temperature, shelter and water are arranged up and down the mountain by elevation. Temperatures are warmest at the bottom of the mountain and coldest at the top. Summer lasts longer at the bottom of the mountain and is shorter at the top. Because of the temperature difference and the length of seasons, plants and animals prefer to live at different elevations. These different elevations are called *life zones*. Within each life zone there are specific plants that live together which are called *communities*. Within the community, rocks, soils, weather conditions, plants and animals all work together. The place where these things work together is called an *ecosystem*.

Note that lowland shrub and forest, montane forest, sublapine forest and alpine tundra can be called either a life zone, which refers to the elevation where these communities occur, or an ecosystem, which refers to the interactions that take place within these communities. Riparian ecosystems, however, are not life zones because they occur at all elevations.

LOWLAND SHRUB AND FOREST

ELEVATION 5,000-8,000 feet above sea level; especially south-facing slopes.

PLANTS Sage, Gambel Oak, Serviceberry, Pinyon Pine, Juniper.

WATER dry like a desert from June-November; snow from November-April; spring water in May.

SUMMER 7 months without snow; food is in the form of seeds, nuts and insects; temperatures are hot; waterholes are dry except for year round creeks, lakes and rivers.

WINTER 5 months of snow, but only 2-3 feet deep; food is in the form of dried shrubs, sage, roots, leftover seeds and nuts; temperatures are freezing at night, but because of shallow snow, many animals can find food here.

MONTANE FOREST

ELEVATION 5,600-9,000 feet above sea level.

PLANTS Aspen trees, Douglas Fir, Lodgepole Pine, Ponderosa Pine, Limber Pine.

WATER seasonal water holes and streams are full from May-June; soil is damp through summer and begins to dry out in August and September; snow covers the ground from November-May.

SUMMER 5-6 months without snow; lots of food; temperatures are warm, not hot; waterholes continue to hold water through early summer.

WINTER 6-7 months of snow up to 5 feet deep in March; food is mostly covered, but birds find seeds and insects, active rodents find seeds, weasels find active rodents; temperatures are freezing.

SUBALPINE FOREST

ELEVATION 9,000-11,400 feet above sea level.

PLANTS Subalpine Fir, Engelman Spruce.

WATER damp soils from June-October, snow cover from October-June.

SUMMER 4-5 months without snow; forests are dark and shady but with plenty of food and water in summer; temperatures are cool.

WINTER 7 8 months of snow up to 10 feet deep in March, most animals migrate lower or hibernate during winter months; animals that remain active in winter are adapted to live with snow and cold.

ALPINE TUNDRA

ELEVATION 12,400-14,433 (the highest point in Colorado) feet above sea level.

PLANTS low-lying grasses, flowers and shrubs.

WATER seasonal water holes in June and July; dry soil from July-October; frozen from October-June.

SUMMER 3 months without snow, but year-round snow fields in some areas; food is in the form of flowering plants, seeds, insects, small rodents; temperatures are cool in the daytime and near freezing at night; be careful when walking through the tundra as it is the most fragile mountain ecosystem.

WINTER 8 months of snow, extreme cold and extreme wind; food is in the form of dried grasses and seeds on the windy side of slopes or on cliff edges where snow is blown free; snow is deepest on the east side of ridges (*leeward side*), shallowest on the western side of ridges (*windward side*) and *cornices* often hang over the eastern side of a ridgeline due to blowing snow.

RIPARIAN ECOSYSTEM

ELEVATION riparian areas are not arranged by elevation. Instead, they occur wherever there is water. Because it can occur at any elevation, a riparian area is always called an ecosystem, not a life zone.

PLANTS Blue Spruce, Narrowleaf Cottonwood (river bottoms), willows (creek beds), Cattail (wetlands).

WATER rivers run fastest, and wetlands and ponds are most full in spring; water is lowest in fall and runs consistently low through the winter, then picks up again in spring as snow melts.

SUMMER lush and green with plenty of food, shelter and water; riparian areas are the most used ecosystem for animal habitat (shelter, migration routes, drinking water, food sources).

WINTER banks are frozen, food is covered, water is frozen on the edges but flowing down the center channels; tall tree trunks still provide shelter for treetop animals.

Lowland Shrub and Forest
Summary

HOT AND DRY

Lowland shrub and forest ecosystems are hot and dry in summer like a desert. Cactus grows here and grasses are dried out by mid-July. Seasonal water holes dry up early in the summer.

ANIMALS

Cottontails, chipmunks and ground squirrels are common in summer. Deer and elk, which are common in winter, migrate upward in summer where it is cooler and where they can find water.

LONG SUMMER

There are usually seven snow-free months. Snow melts by mid-April and starts accumulating again in mid-November.

FOOD

Squirrels, chipmunks and birds eat seeds, leaves, grasses, flowers, nuts and insects. Fox, coyote, bobcat and badger eat squirrels, chipmunks and birds.

LOWLAND SHRUB PLANTS

Gambel Oak in winter and leaf

Sage

family field guide

Lowland Shrub and Forest
Winter

WINTER HABITAT

Winter is cold, but with less than 3 feet of snow on the ground, deer, elk and bighorn sheep use lowland shrub and forests as winter habitat.

SNOW

Snow is on the ground from November through April, but is usually less than 3 feet deep. Deer, elk and bighorn sheep are able to *browse* on shrubs under the snow.

ANIMALS

Chipmunks and ground squirrels hibernate through winter, but mice, pocket gophers and cottontails remain active. Bobcat, badger, coyote and fox eat these animals. Mountain lions migrate here from the montane forests to feed on deer.

LOWLAND FOREST PLANTS

Pinyon Pine tree and cone   Juniper tree and berries

family field guide

Montane Forest
Summer

COOL AND WET

Daytime temperatures are usually warm enough to wear a t-shirt in summer, but evenings are cool. Creeks and springs usually flow through the summer months.

AUTUMN LEAVES

Aspen leaves turn a brilliant gold in fall. When and how sudden the color change occurs depends on seasonal temperatures and rainfall.

ANIMALS

Most Rocky Mountain mammals are here throughout the summer. Bears, ground squirrels and chipmunks wake from *hibernation* in April. Deer, elk and bighorn sheep return from the lowland shrub and forest in May.

MONTANE FOREST PLANTS

Aspen trees: summer

Aspen trees: fall

Aspen trees: winter

family field guide

Montane Forest
Winter

FOOD

Most food types are buried by snow. Seeds, nuts, evergreen needles and insect eggs are enough to feed deer mice, snowshoe hare and pine squirrels which feed the weasels, martens, foxes and coyotes. Many animals, however, migrate to the lowland shrubs or hibernate.

SNOW

Snow begins accumulating by November and may be 5 feet deep in March. Most snow melts by the end of May.

MOUNTAIN TOWNS

Montane forests include aspen groves and low elevation evergreen forests. Ski towns are usually located in or around montane forests.

MONTANE FOREST PLANTS

Ponderosa Pine tree and needles

Douglas Fir trees and cone

Subalpine Forest
Summer

A SUMMER HOME

These high-mountain evergreen forests are dark and shady. Snow lasts long into the summer, but once it melts, there is food, shelter and water to support many types of wildlife.

BE PREPARED

When hiking or camping in subalpine forests, always be prepared for cold temperatures and rain storms. Carry a rain jacket and warm clothes in case of cold weather.

ANIMALS

Like the montane forest, most all of the mammals are here in summer, but they usually don't arrive or wake up until the snow is nearly melted (as late as July).

SUBALPINE FOREST PLANTS

Subalpine Fir and its silver-barked trunk

Engelmann Spruce tree and cones

family field guide

Subalpine Forest
Winter

WATER STORAGE

Subalpine forests act like a reservoir of water. Water collects as snow and is held by cold termperatures. As spring approaches, water is released slowly, providing several months of steady water flow.

STEEP AND DEEP

Snow begins collecting in October, can be 10 feet or more in some areas by the end of April and usually melts by late June.

KRUMMHOLZ

The name *Krummholz* means twisted tree and describes the dwarf trees at timberline. These trees are short because they only have 3 months to grow each season. They appear twisted because strong winds only allow needles to grow on the sheltered side of the tree.

TIMBERLINE

Trees cannot grow if the summer is too short. The elevation where trees stop growing is called *timberline*. Timberline in Colorado is 11,400 feet above sea level.

SUBALPINE FEATURES

Krummholz at timberline

Timberline at 11,400 feet

family field guide

Alpine Tundra
Summer

Lightning storms kill people! When hiking, be aware of fast-moving afternoon storms and get down to the forest before they strike!

SHORT AND SLOW

Snow in the alpine tundra is mostly melted by July and begins collecting again in October; plants only have 3 months to grow.

ANIMALS

Pika, marmot and mountain goat live here all summer while fox, coyote, deer and elk pass through. Most migrating animals do not stay here long because there is limited shelter in this treeless environment.

HARSH ENVIRONMENT

The alpine tundra is the coldest, windiest and driest Rocky Mountain ecosystem. Water is frozen through winter, then melts and flows downhill.

ALPINE TUNDRA FEATURES

Talus Slope slopes covered by large rocks, sometimes hundreds of feet deep.

Scree Field slopes covered with small rocks that slide easily.

family field guide

Alpine Tundra
Winter

Temperatures are so cold and winds are so strong that only the mountain goat, pika and pocket gopher survive and thrive here in winter.

CORNICE

Snow drifts called *cornices* often hang over the edge of mountain ridges. These drifts are created by winds that constantly blow snow in the same direction so that it makes the shape of a wave.

WINDWARD SIDE

In Colorado, winds usually blow from the west towards the east. The west-facing sides of mountains and trees get hammered by wind. This windy side is called the *windward side*. Trees on this side are usually shorter and snow is usually less deep because it is blown away by the wind.

LEEWARD SIDE

Winds in Colorado move from the west. East facing hills are protected from the wind. This protected side is call the *leeward side*. Snow is deeper on this side because it blows over from the windward side and builds up here.

ALPINE TUNDRA FEATURES

Leeward, cornice and windward

Snow blown clear off the windward side

Riparian Ecosystem
Summer

A riparian ecosystem includes the plants, animals, soils and rocks on the land next to rivers, lakes, ponds, creeks and within wetlands.

SPRING FLOODS

Many of the plants growing along the edges of rivers, streams and lakes need spring floods to grow.

SPRING WARNING

As temperatures rise in spring, snow melts and water is added to the rivers, creeks, wetlands and lakes. Be careful around creeks and rivers during spring runoff; water is moving very fast, is very strong and can be very dangerous!

RIPARIAN AREAS

Cottonwood river bank

Cattail marsh

Colorado Blue Spruce river bank

family field guide

Riparian Ecoystem
Winter

Unlike other ecosystems in the mountains, riparian ecosystems do not depend on elevation. Riparian ecosystems flow through all other ecosystems from alpine tundra down to lowland shrubs and forests.

WETLAND

Wetlands are areas of shallow water and are usually muddy, swampy and thick with plants. Wetlands clean the water, absorb water which helps prevent flooding, provide protection for baby animals, provide nesting areas and materials for nesting birds and provide migration pathways too.

LAND OF MANY USES

Biologists estimate that 72% of reptiles, 77% of amphibians, 80% of mammals and 90% of birds that regularly occur in Colorado use riparian ecosystems for food, cover, water or migration routes.

RIPARIAN AREAS

Meandering creek valley

Willows in winter

Mammals

WHAT DO THEY ALL HAVE IN COMMON?

There are over 4,000 different kinds of mammals in the world. Some are big, some are small, some live in water, others on land and some walk, while others fly. Among all of the differences between mammals, they all share the following five characteristics:

LIVE BIRTHS

Most all mammals grow inside the mother before they are born. Humans grow for 9 months before being born, elephants grow for 2 years! Platypuses and two species of echidna are the only mammal babies that grow inside an egg.

MAMMARY GLANDS

When baby mammals are born, most all of them drink milk from their mothers' mammary glands. Birds, on the other hand, eat insects that their mothers have caught, eaten and thrown up for the baby to eat!

WARMBLOODED

No matter the air temperature outside, mammal body temperatures stay the same all the time (except during hibernation). For example, even when the temperature outside is 30 degrees, the human body temperature remains 98.6 degrees.

HAIR

All mammals have hair. Most mammals' hair is obvious like on bears, coyotes and raccoons. Humans have far less hair, but we all have some. Whales and dolphins are born with hair, but then it mostly falls out. They continue to have hair follicles where the hair once grew.

TEETH

All mammals have different types of teeth which have important functions. Canine teeth are used for ripping, molars are used for crushing and incisors (front teeth) are used for slicing or snipping. The fancy word for having different kinds of teeth all in the same mouth is called *heterodont dentition*.

WHAT DO THEY ALL HAVE IN COMMON?

Besides live births, hair, mammary glands, teeth and being warmblooded, all mammals must respond to the threats and parts of their life cycle that influence their behavior.

PREDATORS

This section lists meat eaters that threaten to kill the animal for food. All *herbivores* except for healthy moose have predators. *Carnivores* are less likely to have predators, but small carnivores like weasel, pine marten and fox can be prey to larger carnivores like bear, coyote and mountain lion.

HUMAN THREATS

This section lists all the ways that humans can threaten individual animals or the entire species of animal. Human threats can be as obvious as hunting and car accidents or less obvious like development of houses and roads in important habitat where animals prefer to live.

MATING SEASON

This section lists when a female can become pregnant. Humans can get pregnant any month of the year, but most mammals only have a few months, a few weeks or even a few days when they can become pregnant.

BIRTH SEASON

This section lists the months when babies are born. Human babies are born 9 months after they start growing inside the mother. This time is called a *gestation period*. Count backwards from the time the babies are born to the mating season to calculate the gestation period, but be careful, some animals don't start growing immediately after the mating season; this is called *delayed implantation*.

LITTER SIZE

This section lists how many babies are born during one birth. The word *litter* only describes births of animals that commonly have more than one baby at a time.

Badger
(American Badger)

WHERE (pastures and meadows)

WHEN

WINTER   FOOD   ROLE

National Park Service

PREDATORS
none

HUMAN THREATS
accidental poisoning, *development*, car accidents

MATING SEASON
July-August

BIRTH SEASON
March-April

LITTER SIZE
1-4 (avg. 2)

FAST DIGGING While the pocket gopher is said to dig the most soil of any Rocky Mountain burrowing mammal, badgers are said to be the fastest diggers. They need to dig fast so they can chase down and eat other burrowing animals. Notice the claws and the shape of the head in the picture: they are built for digging!

RODENT CONTROL With its short front legs, long claws and flat body shape, badgers are built to live below ground. They listen for the scratching sounds of burrowing animals, smell for the scent of nesting animals and spend most of each night hunting in underground tunnels eating whatever rodents are in their path. If the badger is not hungry, it will kill its prey and store it in a separate den for later eating.

WICKED AS A WEASEL Badger, pine marten, long-tailed weasel, short-tailed weasel, mink and skunk are all in the weasel family. They all eat meat, they all mark their territories with scent markings and they are all very aggressive fighters. Badgers have thick skin, hair that pulls loose when tugged on and an aggressive fight that can defend against a pair of coyotes--animals five times their size and weight. That's like a fourth grader bullying the world's largest professional wrestler!

family field guide

HABITAT

FOOD pocket gophers, ground squirrels, *voles*, deer mice, cottontails, ground-nesting birds and eggs.

SHELTER underground burrows with one or two rooms extending off a main tunnel; openings are oval-shaped, the size of a football.

WATER mostly from their prey.

RANGE ½ - 1 square mile with several dens in that area.

BUILT FOR DIGGING

The badger,s body is no wider than its head so it can squeeze into small spaces. By comparison, our shoulders are wider than our head so we do not move easily through caves or tunnels.

HEAD

Badgers have a flat head, tiny ears and little eyes which pass easily through football-sized tunnels.

CLAWS

Up to three inches long, their claws are built for digging! Killing prey happens with the teeth.

family field guide

Beaver

WHERE

WHEN

WINTER

FOOD

ROLE

mount courtesy of Cabela's retail store, Kansas City, KS

PREDATORS
coyote, bear, mountain lion

HUMAN THREATS
development, nuisance killing

MATING SEASON
November-March

BIRTH SEASON
May-June

LITTER SIZE
1-4 (avg. 3)

TAIL Beavers slap their tail to warn others of danger. The tail is also used for swimming and to store fat for warmth.

EYES Clear eyelids called *nictitating membranes* close like swim goggles for underwater vision.

REAR FEET Webbed feet allow fast swimming.

FRONT FEET Flexible fingers help hold, grip and place logs and branches.

TEETH Beaver teeth grow constantly and need to be used or they will grow into the skull.

ENGINEERS Look in any creek bottom and notice how beavers alter their environment with dams, canals, downed logs and trails. Their engineering lifestyle helped them become the mascot for the Massachusetts Institute of Technology, a top engineering university in the country.

RETURN FROM NEAR EXTINCTION Trappers moved to the rivers and lakes of Canada, Alaska and the western United States to collect and sell beaver pelts (furs) in the 1800s. Trappers traded pelts in return for supplies. The pelts were then sold and used to make hats. Around 1870, silk became the more fashionable material for hats, so trapping slowed and beaver populations have grown ever since.

family field guide

HABITAT

FOOD   tree bark from aspen, willow and cottonwood.

SHELTER   igloo-shaped *lodge* built with sticks.

WATER   drinks from the pond where it makes its home.

RANGE   adults remain in the same lodge and pond, rarely moving more than 100 yards away from the water; 2-year olds leaving the parents lodge may travel up to ten miles to find their own territory!

LODGE

The entrance is under water so that predators cannot come inside, but their living space is a safe and dry home.

DAMS

Branches, mud and vegetation are laid across streams and creeks to create a dam. A pond fills behind the dam which protects them from predators.

CHEWED TREES

Trees are cut and used for dams and lodges, bark is eaten for food.

Bighorn Sheep
(Mountain Sheep)

SUMMER	SUMMER	SUMMER	WINTER

WHEN	WINTER

FOOD	ROLE

photo by Garry Pfaffmann

A SYMBOL A symbol of the majestic Rocky Mountains, the bighorn sheep was selected as Colorado's state animal in 1961. In the 1800s, when most game animals were over-hunted, the state banned hunting of bighorn sheep to allow the population to grow. In 2006, Colorado has the largest bighorn sheep population in the country.

MAGNIFICENT HORNS Horns are made of keratin, the same material that makes our fingernails. They do not shed each year the way antlers do. Both males and females have horns, but males are much bigger and are more curved. A set of full-grown ram horns can weigh as much as all of the bones in the ram's body combined (over 30 pounds). Scientists look at horns to learn about age and health.

BUILT FOR COMBAT When rams fight for a ewe in the fall, each ram runs toward the other at speeds up to 20 miles per hour. That's like running your head into a brick wall at 40 miles per hour! Ram skulls have extra strong bone structure so they don't crack and an extra tendon connects their skull to their spine so their heads can absorb the powerful blow.

ESCAPE Bighorn sheep feed in flat grassy areas including meadows, creek beds and along highways, but they are always near rocky cliffs which they use as escape routes from predators.

PREDATORS
mountain lion, coyote; bobcat and eagles kill lambs

HUMAN THREATS
hunting, car accidents

OTHER THREATS
lungworm-pneumonia

MATING SEASON
November-December

BIRTH SEASON
May-June

BABIES BORN EACH SEASON
1

family field guide

HABITAT

FOOD *graze* on grasses in summer, *browse* on shrubs in winter.

SHELTER none; migrate to lower elevations in winter.

WATER from plants and streams in summer and snow in winter.

RANGE summer and winter ranges are 3-10 square miles, migrations are only 3-10 miles.

LEAPIN' LIZARDS

Bighorns can jump up to 20 feet from one rock to the next without losing their balance.

NAMES

Males: Ram
Females: Ewe
Young: Lamb

HORN SIZE

Most rams are unable to mate until they are 7 years old when their horns are full grown because they are un-able to win the ewes from the stronger males.

Black Bear

WHEN

WINTER   **FOOD**

ROLE

photo by Robin Henry

PREDATORS
none

HUMAN THREATS
car accidents, *nuisance killing*, hunting

MATING SEASON
June-July

BIRTH SEASON
January-February

LITTER SIZE
2-3 (avg. 2)

WINTER BIRTHS Cubs are born in the middle of winter. At birth, they are the size of an apple, and are blind and without hair. They nurse for two months while their mother sleeps. In spring, when the mother wakes, she and her 20-pound cub begin feeding on grasses, leaves and flesh of animals which have died in winter.

PROBLEM BEARS In fall and spring, bears often feed in towns and campsites where they find plenty of food. Once a bear finds a good feeding ground, it will return to that place and teach cubs to return as well. When a bear becomes comfortable finding food in campsites or houses, it is labeled a *problem bear* because it can be dangerous to people and pets. Problem bears are tranquilized and moved by helicopter at least 50 miles away from the area. If they return to the campsites or neighborhoods they are killed. (Bears have been known to return over 200 miles to their favorite feeding places!)

PROTECT YOURSELF AND BEARS Keep dog food, garbage and bird feeders inside at night during spring, summer and fall!

family field guide

HABITAT

FOOD grasses, roots, flowers, acorns, insects, honey, small rodents, dead animals, berries, occasionally baby deer or elk.

SHELTER winter dens are under trees or cliffs; rest at the base of trees or in treetops in summer.

WATER streams, lakes and food.

RANGE varies from 5 to 75 square miles with daily movements of about ½ mile.

DON'T RUN

Bears can run up to 20 miles per hour for short distances. If you see a bear, stand still, raise your arms, make noise, DON'T RUN!

TORPOR

Scientists call a bear's sleep *torpor*. They can go 200 days without food while their breathing and heart rates slow, but unlike true hibernation, their body temperature remains warm.

FAT FARM

In autumn, a bear has to gain up to 1.5 pounds each day to get fat enough for winter torpor.

NAMES
Male: Boar
Female: Sow
Young: Cub

Bobcat

SUMMER ONLY   WINTER/SUMMER

WHEN   WINTER

FOOD   ROLE

mount courtesy of ACES

PREDATOR
mountain lion

HUMAN THREATS
nuisance killing, hunting

MATING SEASON
February-March

BIRTH SEASON
April-May

LITTER SIZE
2-3

BEWARE Bobcats *camouflage* into shadows of trees and brush. If you mistakenly walk too near, they may growl at you. Their growl is so deep and loud that it is often mistaken as a mountain lion!

BORN TO HUNT Bobcats are adapted to hunt. They camouflage in forest shadows, both eyes are in front of their head so they can focus on their prey and they live alone so they are quieter in their hunt. As with all predators, bobcats have few natural enemies.

RELATIVES The bobcat's scientific name is *Lynx rufus* (red lynx). As you may guess, the lynx is its closest relative. Both cats have tufts of hair on their ears, have spotty coats and like to eat *lagomorphs* (rabbits and hares). Bobcats, however, are smaller and prefer to live in lowland shrub ecosystems where cottontails are common. Lynx are bigger and have huge paws for walking through snow in the subalpine forests where snowshoe hares are common.

FAST TRAINING Babies nurse from their mother for two weeks after birth; then the mother brings birds, mice and cottontails for them to eat. Within six weeks of birth, babies join their mother in hunting. Ten months after birth, they are ready to live on their own, catching every meal they will ever eat for the rest of their lives.

family field guide

HABITAT

FOOD cottontails (30-70% of their diet), ground squirrels, mice, pocket gophers, porcupines, small birds, young deer and elk, domestic sheep, goats and chickens.

SHELTER cracks in rocks or hollow logs for dens when nursing.

WATER streams, lakes, rivers, blood from prey.

RANGE 9-20 square miles for males; females use only 3-10 square miles depending on food.

SMALL KITTY

Bobcats are only as tall as an adult's knees (2 feet) and weigh as much as a computer (15 pounds), but don't be fooled by their small size; bobcats are very aggressive and very good hunters.

NAMED BY ITS TAIL

The name bobcat may come from its short, or "bobbed", tail which is black on top and white near the body. Compare it to the lynx's tail (page 48).

EAR TUFTS

Similar to lynx, but tufts of hair growing on each ear are smaller.

Chipmunk
(Least Chipmunk)

photo by Robin Henry

WHERE

WHEN   **WINTER**

FOOD   **ROLE**

PREDATORS

hawks, owls, fox, coyote, bobcat, marten, weasel, badger

HUMAN THREATS

deforestation, pets

MATING SEASON

April-June

BIRTH SEASON

May-July

LITTER SIZE

4-6

AN AMAZING CHIPMUNK The least chipmunk is the smallest of the 13 different kinds of chipmunks in Colorado. It also lives in more parts of Colorado and in more types of ecosystems than any other Colorado chipmunk.

FOOD FOR OTHERS Like other small rodents, chipmunks are especially important because they are food for many different predators. While many chipmunks are eaten each year, a dozen or so of them are born from each female, so the newly born replace those that are eaten. If predators did not keep their populations small, rodent populations would boom and dangerous side effects would occur.

ECOTONE Least chipmunks prefer to live in sunny areas where they can easily watch for predators. They also like to live near trees or shrubs which provide shelter for hiding. Such areas where two different ecosystems meet (a sunny meadow next to a shaded forest) are called *ecotones* and are favorite living places for wildlife because they provide both food, in meadows, and protection, in forests.

PLEASE DON'T FEED ME Least chipmunks are very common around campsites and they are not afraid to eat your food. Human food, however, is not healthy for wildlife or for people. Chipmunks are not built to digest human food so it can make them sick. Also, once they become accustomed to eating human food, they may beg for food or even sneak into peoples' food storage to steal it.

family field guide

HABITAT

FOOD seeds (50% of diet), berries, flowers, leaves, stems, insects and carrion if available.

SHELTER underground dens beneath rocks and roots at forest edge or in rocky areas.

WATER from their food.

RANGE 2-3 football fields, depending on food.

TORPOR

Like bears, chipmunks sleep through winter, but they wake up every few weeks to feed from their hidden food supply.

SIZE

Least chipmunks are only as large as a baseball.

CHEEKS

Chipmunks have large cheeks for carrying food to and from their food storage.

DIFFERENCES

Least chipmunk stripes pass through the eyes. Golden-mantled ground squirrel stripes start at the shoulder.

least chipmunk   golden-mantled ground squirrel

Cottontail
(Mountain Cottontail or Nuttal's Cottontail)

photo by Garry Pfaffmann

WHEN   WINTER

FOOD   ROLE

PREDATORS
badger, fox, coyote, owls, hawks, eagle, weasel, marten, bobcat, mountain lion

HUMAN THREATS
pets, hunting

MATING SEASON
March-July

BIRTH SEASON
April-September

LITTER SIZE
4-5 litters; 4-5 babies each litter

RABBITS AND HARES Cottontails are rabbits, not hares. Rabbits are born without fur, unable to see for the first week and families live together in underground dens. The fancy word for these helpless babies is *altricial*. Human babies are altricial. Hares, like the snowshoe hare and the jackrabbit, are born with fur, are able to see and adults live alone in simple above-ground nests. The fancy word for babies that are born able to see and run around is *precocial*.

POPULATION CONTROLS When there is a water shortage and less food is available, fewer cottontails are born so that the limited food supply will last longer. In normal years, however, cottontails produce 4-5 litters of babies so that enough animals are born in early summer when predators need the most food, and then several more litters are born in late summer and fall so that enough animals survive winter to reproduce in spring.

LAGOMORPHS Hares and rabbits have large front teeth for eating grasses and nibbling trees just like rodents. Hares, rabbits and pika, however, are not rodents. They are in a family called *lagomorphs* which have two sets of upper front teeth, one large pair in front which they use for nibbling, and a second, small set of peg-like teeth behind them. These pegs are not used for anything, but rabbits, hares and pika have them and rodents do not.

family field guide

HABITAT

FOOD grasses in spring, summer and fall; seeds, sage, leaves, juniper berries and needles in winter.

SHELTER use dens that other animals have dug and abandoned while nursing young, then line the den with fur to make it soft and warm.

WATER mostly from the grasses they eat.

RANGE 1-10 football fields.

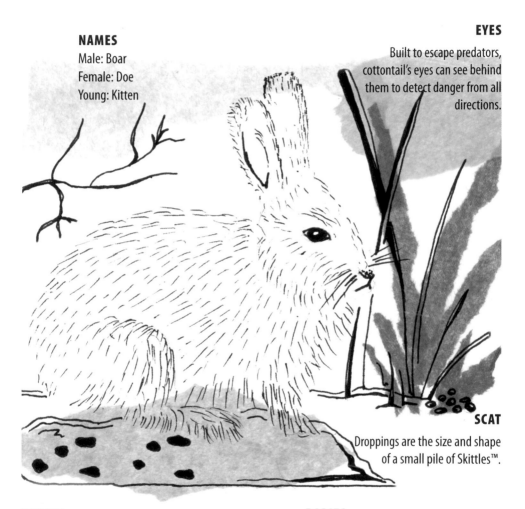

NAMES
Male: Boar
Female: Doe
Young: Kitten

EYES
Built to escape predators, cottontail's eyes can see behind them to detect danger from all directions.

SCAT
Droppings are the size and shape of a small pile of Skittles™.

TRACKS

The back feet land in front of the front feet when they are running, so don't be confused about the direction of travel when looking at tracks.

BABIES

Cottontails are food for so many predators that they have to produce a lot of babies or they would all be eaten. A single female can have 15-20 babies each year!

Coyote

WHEN

WINTER   FOOD

ROLE

photo by Robin Henry

PREDATORS
none

HUMAN THREATS
hunting, poisoning, car accidents

MATING SEASON
January-March

BIRTH SEASON
April-May

LITTER SIZE
4-8 (avg. 6)

THEY'RE EVERYWHERE Coyotes live throughout the United States except in the South and on the East Coast. They live in all of Colorado's ecosystems. They are common in pastures, shrublands, towns, forests, riparian areas and alpine tundra. Wherever there are rodents and/or lago-morphs, coyotes will follow.

WINTER FOOD In winter, coyotes migrate to lower eleva-tions where there is less snow. The shallow snow depth lets them smell, hear and chase deer mice and pocket gophers that live under the snow. Once they hear or smell food, they leap and pounce on their prey. They don't walk well in deep snow, but they sometimes follow ski or snowmobile tracks into montane and subalpine forests where they hunt snow-shoe hare.

COYOTE COMPETITION Coyote populations are large partly because they do not have enough competition. Mountain lions are the only other large predator since griz-zly bears and gray wolves are extinct in Colorado.

WYLIE COYOTE Ranchers have tried poisoning and hunt-ing coyotes as a way of protecting young cows and sheep. When stressed, however, coyotes have more pups in each litter and start having babies at a younger age. As a re-sult, more coyotes survive each year when populations are stressed. No matter how much hunting and poisoning goes on, coyote populations remain stable.

family field guide

HABITAT

FOOD (90% meat) squirrels, cottontails, deer mice, ground-nesting birds, chipmunks, ground squirrels, beaver, young or weak deer and elk, dead animals, garbage, insects, berries.

SHELTER use dens mostly when raising pups.

WATER drink from streams, blood from prey.

RANGE residents who live and hunt with a family need only 10 square miles with winter migrations up to 20 miles to winter habitat; lone *transients* may hunt up to 50 square miles.

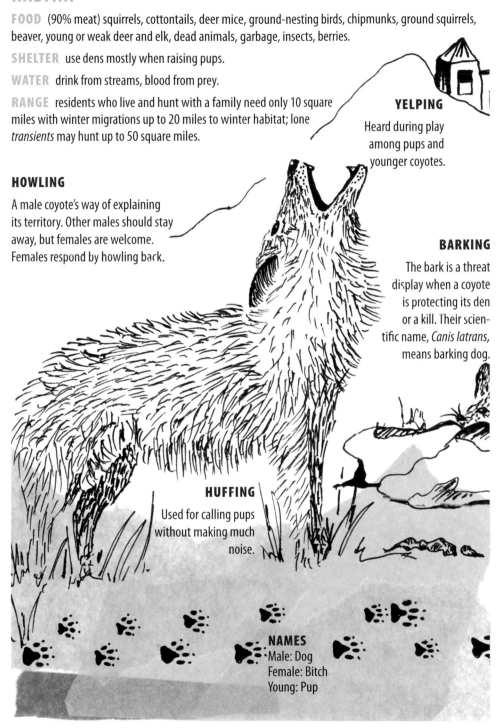

YELPING

Heard during play among pups and younger coyotes.

HOWLING

A male coyote's way of explaining its territory. Other males should stay away, but females are welcome. Females respond by howling back.

BARKING

The bark is a threat display when a coyote is protecting its den or a kill. Their scientific name, *Canis latrans*, means barking dog.

HUFFING

Used for calling pups without making much noise.

NAMES
Male: Dog
Female: Bitch
Young: Pup

Deer Mouse

WHEN   **WINTER**

FOOD   **ROLE**

National Park Service

PREDATORS
owls, weasels, fox, marten, mink, skunk, raccoon, snakes, coyote, large fish, pine squirrel and ground squirrels

HUMAN THREATS
mouse traps, poisoning, pets

MATING SEASON
April-August

BIRTH SEASON
May-September

LITTER SIZE
2-8 mice per litter, 4-5 litters each year

HOW MANY ARE THERE? There are 32 different kinds of deer mice in the world, but all have a similar look and behavior. Biologists estimate that there are more deer mice in North America than any other type of mammal.

BREEDING Deer mice are an important food source for many predators. To survive as a species, many deer mice are born each year so that one or two will survive to have babies the next year. A female will have 2-8 babies in each litter and will have a litter every month throughout the summer. Unlike other rodents, a deer mouse can become pregnant when it is 2 months old and will have its first litter of babies 30 days later. The deer mouse's ability to give birth within the same summer that it is born creates huge populations of deer mice and good winter food supply for predators.

HANTAVIRUS Deer mice are not potty trained. They pee and poop on counters and tables and wherever they please! A tiny virus called hantavirus lives in the urine and droppings of deer mice. If a person vacuums, sweeps or scrubs up the mess, the virus may drift into the air, the person may inhale it and become very sick or even die! Deer mouse droppings must be sprayed with bleach before cleaning and a nose and mouth mask must be worn while cleaning deer mouse droppings and urine! People most commonly suffer from hantavirus below 6,000 feet elevation.

family field guide

HABITAT

FOOD seeds (70-75% of diet), grasses, mushrooms, insect eggs and larvae, bone, dead animals, berries.

SHELTER nest in wood piles, under logs, in thick brush, leaves or hollow logs; live under snow or in buildings in winter.

WATER mostly from their food.

RANGE ½ football field.

COLORS

Deer mice are tan on top with white undersides, similar to the color of white-tailed deer from which they get their name.

SUBNIVEAN (BELOW THE SNOW)

Deer mice live under the snow in winter where the temperature is always 32 degrees with no wind!

TRACKS

In winter, deer mouse tracks are easy to identify with the dragging tail.

family field guide

Elk

SUMMER   SUMMER   SUMMER   WINTER

WHEN   WINTER

FOOD   ROLE

Elk bull and cows

PREDATORS
coyote, mountain lion

DISEASE
chronic wasting disease

HUMAN THREATS
hunting, car accidents, development

MATING SEASON
September-October

BIRTH SEASON
May-June

BABIES BORN EACH SEASON
1

PREDATORS Gray wolves and grizzly bears were important predators in Colorado's mountains, but both are now extinct in the the state. While mountain lion and coyote prey on young elk, hunting is the main way of managing elk populations since two important predators are gone.

POPULATIONS Colorado has the largest elk population in the United States. Two hundred years ago, elk lived in all of the mainland United States except Arkansas and Florida. As people began moving west, hunters killed elk in large numbers and sold them as food. Elk moved from grazing the open plains with buffalo to hiding in the mountains. Even in the mountains they were still hunted nearly to extinction. Colorado's population was so small that elk were moved from Wyoming to Colorado in the early 1900s. The population has grown ever since.

MATING DISPLAYS The fall mating season is called the *rut*. Elk are most interesting to watch in September and October when they are in their rut. Listen for the male's *bugle*, a call used to attract females. Dozens of females may follow the sound, but they only mate with the strongest male. Males, then, use their antlers to fight each other and the winner gets to mate with the *harem* of females. The male will stay with the females through December, then leaves them and lives alone through the winter. Females live in herds through the winter.

family field guide

HABITAT

FOOD *graze* on grass in summer, *browse* on shrubs in winter.

SHELTER hide under trees for protection from wind and rain; migrate to lower elevation in winter.

WATER streams, ponds, lakes, food and snow.

RANGE summer range for females is 3-10 square miles and 5-20 square miles for males; winter migrations range from 5-35 miles.

ANTLERS

A pair of full-grown antlers weighs 20-30 pounds. A large rack may have six *tines* or *points* on each antler. In rare occasions a set will have 7, 8 or even 9 points on each antler. Antlers are *shed* in March or April and begin growing immediatley.

TREE CHEWS

Elk eat bark in winter when other foods are covered in snow. They have no upper front teeth and leave two vertical scars where they scrape the bark off with their lower teeth.

SCAT

Small piles of Junior Mint™-sized droppings most of the year, but wet patties in spring.

NAMES

Male: Bull
Female: Cow
Young: Calf

TRACKS

The size of an eight-year-old's hand, elk tracks point in the direction of travel.

family field guide

Golden-Mantled Ground Squirrel

WHERE

WHEN   **WINTER**

FOOD   **ROLE**

PREDATORS
hawks, owls, fox, coyote, marten, weasel, badger, bobcat, mountain lion

HUMAN THREATS
pets

MATING SEASON
April-May

BIRTH SEASON
May-June

LITTER SIZE
2-8 (avg. 5)

WARM AND SUNNY These rodents live in open areas with good visibility and a few trees and rocks for shelter. Unlike the least chipmunk, these ground squirrels do not venture into forests. They like grassy meadows, but do not live with Wyoming ground squirrels.

TORPOR These ground squirrels sleep most of the year. They begin their winter nap in October, a few weeks before the chipmunks and they wake up in April or May, depending on temperatures and snow. They wake up often in winter to snack from their food stash, then go back to sleep, but only for one to two weeks at a time between feedings.

WHAT'S THE DIFFERENCE? Golden-mantled ground squirrels and least chipmunks look similar, but can be easily distinguished. The most obvious is that a chipmunk's stripes pass through the face and golden-mantled ground squirrel stripes do not pass through the face. Also, golden-mantled ground squirrels are bigger and fatter than chipmunks.

Least chipmunk   Golden-mantled ground squirrel

family field guide

HABITAT

FOOD seeds, leaves, stems, fungi, insects, bird eggs and young.

SHELTER underground dens beneath rocks and roots in forests, usually near open, sunny areas.

WATER from plants.

RANGE 2-30 football fields.

DO NOT FEED

Golden-mantled ground squirrels are common in campsites and they are not afraid to take your food. Eating human food, however, can make wildlife sick, so be careful that they do not eat your food!

STRIPES

These stripes are obvious and they start at the shoulder.

CHEEKS

Golden-mantled ground squirrels have large cheeks so that they can carry food to their food storage.

Lynx

Colorado Division of Wildlife

PREDATORS
mountain lion and coyote

HUMAN THREATS
illegal hunting, development, cars

MATING SEASON
March-May

BIRTH SEASON
May-July

LITTER SIZE
1-6 (avg. 3)

SECRETIVE BY NATURE Like most cats, lynx hunt alone. They depend on silence and secrecy for their sneak attack hunting style. They usually stalk their prey from the ground but sometimes hide in trees and pounce down. Scientists estimate that lynx catch their prey 36 times out of every 100 attacks.

REINTRODUCTION Colorado has been the southernmost part of lynx range, but they were listed as endangered in Colorado in 1976. No confirmed tracks, scat or sightings were recorded from 1973-1999. In January 1999, 41 lynx were trapped from Canada and introduced to southern Colorado; 55 more were introduced in 2000. The released animals wear collars with satalite transmissions so that biologists can track them. Of the first 96 lynx released, 45 died due to starvation, illegal hunting and car accidents. In the spring of 2005, 16 dens and 46 kittens were found and 34 females were identified with 23 possible mating pairs. More offspring are alive but uncollared. Most supporters call the reintroduction a success.

UNWANTED COMPETITON Snowmobiles and backcountry skiers pack trails that lead into subalpine forests. Fox and coyote use these trails and are now able to hunt in deep snowy places. Lynx have only recently had winter hunting competition as fox and coyote now follow recreationists into lynx winter range.

HABITAT

FOOD snowshoe hare (80% of their diet), birds, pine squirrels, mice, ground squirrels, beaver, muskrat, young deer and elk, sheep.

SHELTER den under ledges, fallen trees or in caves; find cover under evergreens in bad weather.

WATER streams, lakes, blood from prey.

RANGE 10-95 square miles depending on food supply; adults avoid each other except during mating season.

EAR TUFTS

Black tufts of hair stick up from the ears. According to the National Wildlife Federation, these ear tufts act as antannae which funnel sound waves into their ears for better hearing.

SIZE

Similar size, tail, ear tufts and color to bobcat, but the lynx's huge feet are different.

FEET

HUGE back feet act as snowshoes in winter and as swimming flippers in summer.

family field guide

Marmot
(Yellow-Bellied Marmot or Whistle Pig)

WHERE (always in rocky areas)

WHEN	WINTER

FOOD	ROLE

photo by John Rushenberg

PREDATORS
golden eagle, badger, fox, bear, coyote, bobcat

HUMAN THREATS
warming temperatures alter hibernation

MATING
April-May

BIRTH SEASON
May-June

LITTER SIZE
3-8 (avg. 4)

WHEN TO SLEEP Generally, marmots begin hibernation in September and wake up in April. Timing, however, depends on snow depth and seasonal temperatures around the marmot's den. Colonies in the alpine tundra begin hibernating earlier and end later than colonies at lower elevations.

HIBERNATION PREPARATION Marmots feed at dawn and again at dusk, then rest on rocks throughout the summer days. Their laziness helps them to store fat which will act as fuel during hibernation to allow their heart to pump, their lungs to breathe and their body temperature to stay above freezing, all without eating any food for 8 months. While marmots are preyed on by many predators, their biggest threat to survival is having the right amount of stored energy to survive through hibernation.

TRUE HIBERNATION VS. TORPOR Marmots are true hibernators. During hibernation their body temperature drops from 89 degrees to 42 degrees, their breathing slows from 100 breaths/minute to 4 breaths/minute and their heart rate drops from 110 beats/minute to 10 beats/minute. By comparison, bears are not considered true hibernators. While a bear's breathing and heart rate slows, its body temperature does not drop dramatically. A true hibernator's breathing, heart rate and body temperature all must drop, otherwise the sleep is called *torpor*.

family field guide

HABITAT

FOOD grasses and flowering plants.

SHELTER burrows over 3 feet deep are dug beneath rocks so predators cannot dig them up; hibernation burrows are at least 10 feet deep. Marmots spend over 80% of their lifetime in their burrow.

WATER 75% of water comes from drinking, 25% from food.

RANGE colonies cover up to 4 football fields in size; males defend up to 2 football fields and all of the females within that area.

ADAPTABILITY

Marmots can live in many different temperatures from the frozen alpine tundra to the hot lowland shrubs as long as they have large fields of boulders to protect their burrow from digging predators.

FEAST AND FAMINE

Before hibernation, half of the marmot's body weight needs to be stored as fat. For example, if you weigh 80 pounds, you would have to gain 40 more pounds before hibernating! Fat is used during hibernation so when marmots wake up in spring they are skinny again!

WHISTLE PIGS

While lazing on rocks, marmots watch for intruders and send warning calls to the rest of the colony. Each animal has a different call so marmots within the colony can identify each other's voices.

Mink
(American Mink)

WHERE

WHEN

WINTER

FOOD

ROLE

National Park Service

PREDATORS
mostly other mink; also coyote, bobcat and owl

HUMAN THREATS
small game hunting/trapping

MATING SEASON
February-April

BIRTH SEASON
April-May

LITTER SIZE
2-6 (avg. 4)

HUNTERS Like all members of the weasel family, mink are specialized hunters. They watch for prey from the shore then dive into the water and chase it down. Mink usually kill more prey than they can eat, then store it for later eating.

A FINE COAT In winter, mink grow a thick coat which allows them to hunt and swim in the coldest temperatures. They produce an oil in glands near their rear end which they spread throughout their fur when they clean themselves. This oil waterproofs their fur.

MINK FARMS Mink skins have been used as clothing by Native American tribes, trappers, explorers and city folk for hundreds of years. In the 1800s people began raising mink in farms around the world. In many places, American mink escaped from their cages and survived in the wild. So many animals have escaped that American mink populations are high throughout much of the world and, because of their aggressive nature, they have displaced the European mink in many areas of Europe.

KNOW BEFORE YOU BUY Mink are wild animals that do not live well in cages. Chickens, cows and horses can survive without stress in a decent sized pen and with responsible handling, but after 200 years of breeding mink still become stressed unless they are allowed to swim and hunt in an open area. Before buying a mink coat, realize that mink are not domesticated animals and that it takes 35-60 of them to make one fur coat.

family field guide

HABITAT

FOOD muskrat, deer mice, cottontails, frogs, slamanders, fish, beaver kits, nestling water birds, insects.

SHELTER use abanadoned muskrat dens along a river or lake bank. Males may have several dens within their territory.

WATER streams and lakes.

RANGE usually 1-3 square miles; males' territories do not overlap because when they meet, they fight, often to the death.

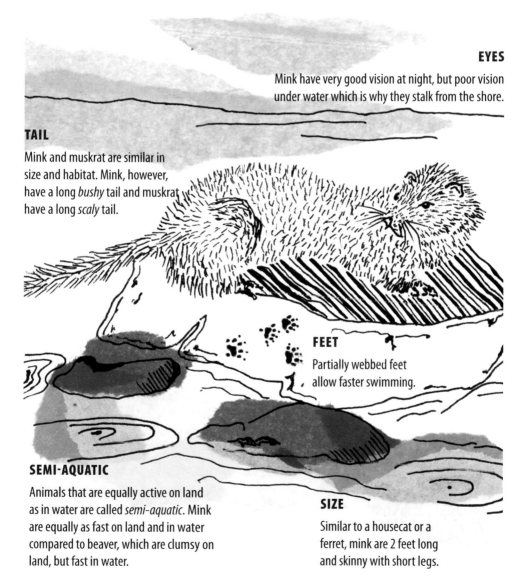

EYES

Mink have very good vision at night, but poor vision under water which is why they stalk from the shore.

TAIL

Mink and muskrat are similar in size and habitat. Mink, however, have a long *bushy* tail and muskrat have a long *scaly* tail.

FEET

Partially webbed feet allow faster swimming.

SEMI-AQUATIC

Animals that are equally active on land as in water are called *semi-aquatic*. Mink are equally as fast on land and in water compared to beaver, which are clumsy on land, but fast in water.

SIZE

Similar to a housecat or a ferret, mink are 2 feet long and skinny with short legs.

family field guide

Moose

WHERE

WHEN

WINTER

FOOD

ROLE

National Park Service

PREDATORS
mountain lion, lynx and coyote kill calves

HUMAN THREATS
limited hunting

MATING SEASON
September-November

BIRTH SEASON
May-June

BABIES BORN EACH SEASON
1

SOUTHERN EXPOSURE Colorado is the southernmost part of moose habitat in the United States. Moose prefer colder climates where snow is deep and they have less competition for winter feeding. Their long legs can easily walk through snow up to 3 feet deep while deer and elk are only comfortable with up to 1-2 feet of snow.

REINTRODUCTION Moose are thought to be native mammals to Colorado that were hunted to extinction in the 1800s. The Colorado Division of Wildlife has trapped moose from Utah and moved them to Colorado on three separate occassions to help increase their population. In the late 1970s moose were introduced to northern Colorado near North Park, in the early 1990s a herd was introduced in southern Colorado near Creede and in 2005 moose were relocated on Grand Mesa near Grand Junction. As moose migrate to find the best habitat, they will be more commonly observed throughout the state. In 2005 a moose was seen near Aspen, over 100 miles from any reintroduction location.

A DIFFERENT DEER Moose, mule deer and elk are all in the deer family. They all have hooves, *shed* and grow new antlers each year and are herbivores. Unlike deer and elk, however, moose rarely form herds, males do not mate with a *harem* of females and moose shed their antlers in early winter instead of spring.

family field guide

HABITAT

FOOD summer grazing of most vegetation in and along waterways, winter browsing of willow and aspen twigs along stream banks.

SHELTER none; grow a winter coat for warmth; may or may not migrate long distances.

WATER streams and ponds where they graze and browse.

RANGE 2-4 square miles; some migrate for calving and winter, others do not.

ANTLER SIZE

Moose antlers can grow 6 feet wide from side to side! Imagine trying to walk through the forest with an adult laying sideways across your head!

ANTLER WEIGHT

Moose antlers may weigh up to 30 pounds each, that's 60 pounds for the set! Imagine carrying two large bowling balls on each side of your head!

LONG LEGS

Legs up to 5 feet long allow moose to walk through deep winter snow.

COLORADO'S BIGGEST

The moose is Colorado's biggest mammal. Males are over 6 feet tall from hoof to shoulder, nearly 7 feet tall to the ear and can weigh up to 1,300 pounds.

family field guide

Mountain Goat

WHERE (always near cliffs)

WHEN   WINTER

FOOD   ROLE

photo by Hilary Forsyth

PREDATORS
coyote, mountain lion, bobcat, bear

HUMAN THREATS
hunting

OTHER THREATS
climbing accidents, avalanches

MATING SEASON
November-December

BIRTH SEASON
May-June

BABIES BORN EACH SEASON
1-2

SECRET TO SUCCESS Mountain goats live in an environment where few other animals can. The cliffs protect them from predators and keep competition away from their isolated food supply.

FOOD SHORTAGE In winter, when food is in short supply, goats graze on the windy side of mountains where high winds blow the snow clear, exposing grasses, shrubs and *lichens*. Also, cliff faces too steep for snow to stick provide slight ledges where grasses and shrubs can be eaten. Goats fight each other to defend these food supplies.

HORNS AND SKIN Male and female mountain goats both have horns about one foot long. The horns are used to fight each other and to defend against predators. When fighting, they spear each other's rump and belly. The larger animal pokes and shoves the weaker animal. Skin on their *hindquarters* is extra thick to protect from pointy horns, but sometimes weaker animals are pushed over cliff ledges to their death.

RELATIVES Mountain goats are not goats and they are not related to deer! They are in the pronghorn family and most closely related to bighorn sheep.

family field guide

HABITAT

FOOD grass, leaves and flowers in summer; trees, shrubs and *lichens* in winter; lick salt from rocks.

SHELTER use cliffs and overhanging rocks for protection; long, thick fur protects them from weather.

WATER mostly from their food.

RANGE 7-15 square miles with winter migration up to 3 miles.

HAIR

Goats grow an incredible winter coat. The short underhairs close to the body are 3 inches long and downy soft. The stringy outer hairs which protect from wind and rain, are up to 7 inches long! Deer hair, by comparison, is only 1-2 inches long.

HORNS

A new ring grows each year on a mountain goat's horns. Like all horns, they never fall off.

LEGS

Strong hind legs help them leap from rock to rock.

HOOVES

With hard edges and a soft center, their hooves can act as hooks to pull up on rocks or as suction cups when stepping straight down.

NAMES

Male: Billy
Baby: Kid
Female: Nannie

family field guide

Mountain Lion

SUMMER

SUMMER

SUMMER

WINTER

WHEN

WINTER

FOOD

ROLE

PREDATORS
none

HUMAN THREATS
car accidents, legal and illegal hunting

MATING SEASON
any time

BIRTH SEASON
summer

LITTER SIZE
1-6 (avg. 2)

MANY PLACES, MANY NAMES Puma, panther, cougar and mountain lion all refer to the same animal. The mountain lion is the largest cat in North America and has the largest range of any North American cat. They live in mountains, deserts and rainforests in southern Canada, western United States, Mexico, Central and South America down to Argentina!

THE HUNT Adult mountain lions eat about 1 deer every two weeks. They quietly stalk their prey until they stand within 50 feet of a kill. They may wait for hours until the prey has let its guard down, then spring forward off of strong hind legs, bounding up to 30 feet in the first lunge. In chase, they run with front legs extended forward trying to trip the prey. Once the prey has fallen, the mountain lion bites the neck (either the spine or the windpipe) for the kill.

ATTACK! A person is more likely to drown in their own bathtub than to be attacked by a mountain lion; however, as people choose to live in mountain lion habitat we need to be aware of safety. Ten people were attacked and 3 people killed in Colorado by mountain lion attacks from 1991-2005. Usually the attacking lions are injured or old animals that can no longer hunt successfully. A more likely concern is to protect your pets from mountain lion attacks by keeping them inside at night.

family field guide

HABITAT

FOOD deer (70% of their diet), young elk and moose, beaver, porcupine, raccoon, birds, small mammals, domestic sheep and calves.

SHELTER use cracks in rocks and hollowed trees for dens when nursing young, otherwise do not use a shelter.

WATER streams, lakes and blood from prey.

RANGE females use 15-250 square miles within a whole year depending on food; males use 45-320 square miles; 10-15 mile movements each day are common.

BE ALERT IN MOUNTAIN LION HABITAT!

Always watch your children when playing outside in mountain lion habitat.

Don't attract deer or raccoons to your yard.

If encountered look big, back off slowly and don't make eye contact.

Keep pets inside at night.

If attacked, fight back.

Be most alert at dusk and dawn and carry pepper spray.

family field guide

Mule Deer

SUMMER

SUMMER

SUMMER

WINTER

WHEN WINTER

WHEN SUMMER

WINTER

FOOD

ROLE

Colorado Division of Wildlife

PREDATORS
coyote, bobcat, bear and mountain lion

HUMAN THREATS
hunting, car accidents, development

MATING SEASON
November-December

BIRTH SEASON
May-June

BABIES BORN EACH SEASON
1-2

BIG, FAST AND HIGH When spooked, a mule deer leaps up to 8 feet into the air, all four legs landing together moving as fast as 25 miles per hour. This way of moving, called *stotting* or *pronking*, is much faster than running through and around bushes and shrubs.

CYCLES AND SEASONS Mule deer live high up on the mountain in spring, summer and fall. In fall, when one foot of snow collects on their summer range, they begin their downward migration to valley bottoms. Over 20 inches of snow buries food too deep to be eaten. Even in lower valleys where snow is less deep, 7 out of every 10 fawns die due to predators, starvation or car accidents. Those that survive migrate back to the same summer range every year.

THE ANTLER CYCLE Antlers are bones that grow from the skull and fall off each year. Mule deer, elk and moose antlers are the fastest growing animal parts in the world. Antlers begin growing in spring and are covered in *velvet*, a soft tissue filled with blood vessels that carry vitamins and minerals to the bone so that it can grow. During the velvet phase, mule deer antlers can grow up to .75 inches each day. By fall, the bone has stopped growing and the velvet begins to shed. Animals scrape their antlers on trees to peel the velvet off. The antlers then are hardened and ready for use. The entire purpose of growing antlers is for fighting during mating season so the strongest males can mate with the females. Mule deer antlers fall off in February or March and begin growing again immediately.

family field guide

HABITAT

FOOD *graze* on grass in summer; *browse* on shrubs in winter.

SHELTER none; grow a thick coat and migrate to lower elevation in winter; bed down under trees during storms.

WATER from streams, lakes, snow and food.

RANGE summer and winter range is 5-10 square miles with winter migrations up to 10 miles.

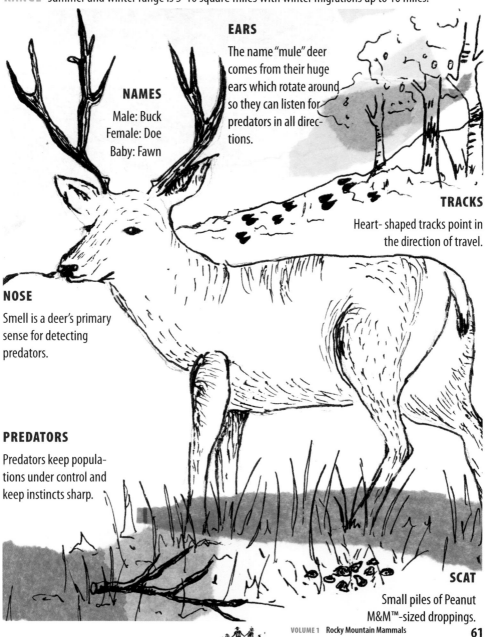

EARS

The name "mule" deer comes from their huge ears which rotate around so they can listen for predators in all directions.

NAMES

Male: Buck
Female: Doe
Baby: Fawn

TRACKS

Heart- shaped tracks point in the direction of travel.

NOSE

Smell is a deer's primary sense for detecting predators.

PREDATORS

Predators keep populations under control and keep instincts sharp.

SCAT

Small piles of Peanut M&M™-sized droppings.

family field guide

Muskrat

WHERE

WHEN

WINTER

FOOD

ROLE

photo by Robin Henry

PREDATORS
mink, raccoon, coyote, fox

HUMAN THREATS
small game hunting/trapping

MATING SEASON
April-July

BIRTH SEASON
May-August

LITTER SIZE
2 litters; 4-8 animals per litter

A TELL-TAIL SIGN Muskrat, beaver and mink can be difficult to tell apart. A muskrat's long, skinny tail slithers fast like a snake when it swims and is easier to see than a beaver's or mink's. A muskrat's tail is scaly like a beaver's, but long and skinny like a mink's.

ESCAPE When frightened, a muskrat can stay under water up to 15 minutes while it swims to its burrow.

A FINE COAT Muskrats have long been trapped for their soft fur coats. Even today, they are trapped more than any other mammal in the United States. Muskrat farms opened in Europe in the late 1800s. Many muskrats escaped and survived in the wild. Now, muskrat populations both in North America and parts of Europe are very healthy.

FRIENDS Muskrat and beaver get along so well that muskrats have been known to share lodges with beaver families. It is very uncommon that two different animal species can share the same home, but beavers and muskrats live in the same environment, do not compete for food (beavers feed on wood and muskrats feed on green plants) and both are herbivores so they do not threaten to eat each other.

family field guide

HABITAT

FOOD roots of aquatic plants, leaves, vegetation, crayfish, frogs, snails, fish and insects.

SHELTER burrows dug into the banks of slow moving rivers or lakes with the entrance below water and the nest above waterline; small cone-shaped lodges of dried plants in marsh areas.

WATER lakes and streams.

RANGE ½ football field.

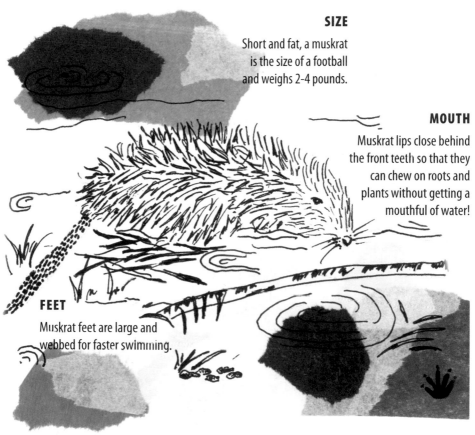

SIZE
Short and fat, a muskrat is the size of a football and weighs 2-4 pounds.

MOUTH
Muskrat lips close behind the front teeth so that they can chew on roots and plants without getting a mouthful of water!

FEET
Muskrat feet are large and webbed for faster swimming.

TAIL
The tail is as long as the rest of its body, has no hair and is vertically flat! The long, skinny tail moves like a snake in the water when swimming.

RELATIVES
Muskrats are large, semi-aquatic *voles*. Voles are mouse-like rodents that live in grasses and thick brush.

family field guide

Pika

WHERE

WHEN

WINTER

FOOD

ROLE

National Park Service

PREDATORS
weasel, marten, eagle, coyote

HUMAN THREATS
possibly warming temperatures (see text)

MATING SEASON
April-June

BIRTH SEASON
May-July

LITTER SIZE
2-4 (avg. 3)

CLIMATE CHANGE Pika have few predators and little competition in the alpine tundra. As global temperatures warm, however, other animals are able to live at higher elevations. As these populations move, competition for food and shelter increase. Some pika populations have disappeared in low alpine areas.

WARNING CALL Pika use their warning call to protect the colony from predators and to defend their territory from other pika. Pika live in groups and depend on each other for security. When a pika senses danger, it sends a warning call so the rest of the colony can scurry towards their dens. The warning call is also used to tell competing pika to go away. Though they live in groups, each pika defends its own territory which it uses to harvest grasses and flowers. Territories are marked with scent marks and urine, and a warning call is used to challenge those who ignore the marks.

STORAGE Unlike most mammals its size, pika do not hibernate in winter. They are awake all winter and continue to eat grass from under the snow, but depend on stored grass and flowers in case food runs out in winter. Pika are busy all summer preparing for the winter food storage and can cut, dry and store up to a bushel of plant material each year. A bushel is enough to fill 8 one-gallon milk jugs (equal to 80 times a pika's body size).

family field guide

HABITAT

FOOD grasses, leaves, flowering plants; collect and dry grass in summer to store in the den for use in winter.

SHELTER use grass and fur to create a den beneath rocks in *scree fields* and *talus slopes*.

WATER vegetation and melting snow.

RANGE ½ football field.

PREDATORS

Warning calls and rocky dens often protect pika from hawks, eagles, coyotes and foxes. Weasels and martens, however, are able to walk right into the dens for an easy meal!

CAMOUFLAGE

Pika use camouflage to hide from predators. They stand still, allowing their color and shape to blend into the rocks.

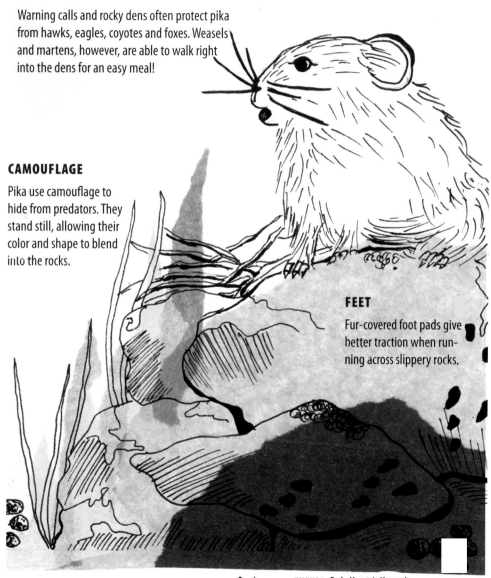

FEET

Fur-covered foot pads give better traction when running across slippery rocks.

family field guide

Pine Marten
(American Marten)

WHEN

WINTER   FOOD   ROLE

National Park Service

PREDATORS
coyote, fox, lynx, mountain lion

HUMAN THREATS
trapping, deforestation

MATING SEASON
July-August

BIRTH SEASON
March-April

LITTER SIZE
2-4 (avg. 3)

TREETOP BANDITS Martens hop from branch to branch as quickly as a pine squirrel. Though they prefer to eat mice and voles, they also prey on pine squirrels, birds and eggs in the treetops as well. Pine martens are the main tree-top predator in Colorado; other mammal carnivores hunt mostly on the ground.

ENERGETIC CHARACTER Martens are fast-moving, fidgety animals, constantly on the move. Their long skinny bodies zig-zag quickly on the ground, up a tree, back down, through thick brush, then to rest in a branch again. They need to eat 2-3 rodents each day to maintain their energetic lifestyle. If a 60-pound child were to eat the same proportion of food, he would need to eat 100 Quarter Pounders™ each day.

WINTER CHANGES Martens are able to survive cold snowy winters because their favorite foods, deer mice, voles and pine squirrels, are all active in winter. Martens are built to sneak under the snow, into dens and up through the treetops to catch their prey. Hair grows between their foot pads in winter to help them float across the snow without sinking.

family field guide

HABITAT

FOOD deer mice and *voles* (70-80 % of the diet), pine squirrel, chipmunk, cottontail, pika, insects, dead animals, berries, birds and eggs.

SHELTER den in hollow trees, fallen timber, woodpecker holes and rocks.

WATER streams, lakes and blood from prey.

RANGE 1-6 square miles; martens hunt their entire territory every 8-10 days and are constantly on the move.

TAILS

The long tail is used to keep balance while hopping, jumping and bouncing through the forest.

TERRITORY

Like all members of the weasel family, martens use scent to mark their territory. It's not as strong as a skunk's, but the smell is noticeable!

A BIG WEASEL

Martens are 2-3 times the size of long-tailed weasels, but their similar shape lets them enter the dens of burrowing rodents.

family field guide

Pine Squirrel
(Chickaree or Red Squirrel)

WHERE

WHEN   WINTER

FOOD   ROLE

photo by Robin Henry

SMALL SQUIRREL Pine squirrel, chickaree, red squirrel and barking squirrel are all names for the same animal, the smallest tree squirrel in Colorado. Colorado's other two tree squirrels, Aberts squirrel and red fox squirrel, are much larger and live only at lower elevations.

TERRITORIAL EXTREMES Pine squirrels are the noisiest defenders of territory in the Rocky Mountain forest. When intruders enter their territory, they perch visibly on branches, voice their warning chatter, flutter their tail restlessly and they do not stop until the intruder is out of sight. The territorial aggression is not saved for predators and competitors alone: except for the two or three days of mating in spring, males and females defend their territories from each other.

FOOD STORAGE Pine squirrels are unique from other squirrels because they do not hibernate. In winter they feed on the seeds inside evergreen cones and on seeds they collected and stored in summer and fall. During summer and fall, they collect food obsessively, taking seeds out of evergreen cones, dropping the leftovers below their feeding tree and stashing the seeds beneath the litter or *midden pile*. Even when the midden piles have enough food stored to supply several generations of squirrels, an individual will continue to collect and store food.

PREDATORS
marten, forest hawks, owls

HUMAN THREATS
deforestation

MATING SEASON
April-June

BIRTH SEASON
May-July

LITTER SIZE
2-5 (avg. 3)

family field guide

HABITAT

FOOD seeds from evergreen cones (80%), berries, leaves, buds, bird eggs and young.

SHELTER nests of leaves and needles in upper branches.

WATER mostly from their food.

RANGE 1-2 football fields in dense evergreen forests, up to 5 football fields in thin forests where food is limited.

ROCKY MOUNTAIN MONKEYS

Pine squirrels are fun to watch as they jump from tree to tree and branch to branch high up in the forest canopy.

TRACKS

Pine squirrel tracks are common in winter. Similar to rabbits and hares pine squirrels have large rear feet, short front feet and hop in a similar pattern.

TAIL

The pine squirrel's tail is equally as long as the rest of the body which gives balance when hopping through tree branches.

CHEEKS

Pine squirrels have oversized cheeks allowing them to carry food to and from their midden pile.

Pocket Gopher
(Northern Pocket Gopher)

WHERE

WHEN

WINTER FOOD ROLE

Surpise! No pocket gopher here. *Eskers* are the most common sign that a pocket gopher has been nearby.

PREDATORS
badger, weasel, coyote, fox, skunk, owl, hawk, bobcat

HUMAN THREATS
cannot burrow in soil that is paved or ploughed

OTHER THREATS
spring floods fill burrows and drown nestlings

MATING SEASON
April-June

BIRTH SEASON
May-June

LITTER SIZE
4-6

THE GOPHER DEN A pocket gopher burrow is a series of underground tunnels, rooms and nests covering up to 200 square yards. Imagine an animal the size of your foot, with paws the size of your pinky, digging the soil out from beneath half a football field.

ESKERS In winter, gophers dig underground, sometimes passing up through the snow, then back down again. As they dig through the snow they create a snow tunnel which fills with soil as they dig back underground. When the snow melts, a cylinder shaped mold of soil remains on the ground. These molds are called *eskers*, a geology term that describes rocks left by glaciers in a similar shape.

FOOD CHAIN Pocket gophers are rarely seen by people and rarely missed by predators. Almost every predator in the area likes to eat them. Weasels wander through their dens, badgers chase them underground, foxes and coyotes spend most of their time listening, sniffing, digging and pouncing on them, and are so clever that they may watch a badger hunt in hopes that the pocket gopher will scurry out of the den so they can slurp up a free meal. Owls are on the watch at night hoping to catch one, too.

family field guide

HABITAT

FOOD roots and tubers in winter; leaves, stems and flowers in summer

SHELTER these complex burrows have separate food storage, bedroom and bathroom and are no more than 3 feet below the ground.

WATER most water comes from plants.

RANGE ½ football field.

TAILS

Hairless tails keep the animal clean and allow it to turn around without brushing soil off the walls.

SMALL EARS

Small ears pass easily through tight tunnels.

TUNNELS

Burrows are usually close to the surface so that they can eat plant roots.

POCKETS

Pocket gophers have two fur-lined "pockets" or pouches, one on each side of their mouth, which allow the gopher to nibble food and store it for later eating.

BUILT TO DIG

One study estimated that a single pocket gopher can move up to 1 ton or 2,000 pounds of soil per year!

LIPS

Their lips close behind their front teeth so that they can chew and keep soil out of their mouth!

Porcupine

FOOD   ROLE

mount courtesy of ACES

PREDATORS
mountain lion, bobcat, coyote

HUMAN THREATS
nuisance killings, car accidents, deforestation

MATING SEASON
September-November

BIRTH SEASON
April-June

NMBER OF BABIES BORN
1-2

MASTER OF PROTECTION When attacked, porcupines raise the quills on their back, turn the tail towards the predator and try to push up against it. The tail quills are loosely attached so that when they touch something, they stick into it. Predators can die if a quill sticks into them and enters a vital organ or if the wound becomes infected!

TREETOPS Porcupines are built to live in the trees. They often rest during the day in rocky dens and feed in trees at night. As their name explains, they prefer pine trees but may feed on other evergreens, cottonwoods or gambel oak, too. Their long claws are built for climbing, the palms and soles have bumpy skin for better traction and their strong tails help brace themselves in the tree branches. Their teeth are covered in an orange-colored enamel that is extra strong for eating wood (same as beaver teeth).

HARD HAIRS Porcupines are known for their quills. Quills are actually hairs that are hardened for protection. They are sharp and barbed, or curved, at the tip so they are difficult to remove once they stick into something. Porcupines have hair around their face mixed with short quills, but around the tail, the quills are as long as an index finger. Fortunately, when porcupines are born, the quills are soft, then harden a few hours after birth.

family field guide

HABITAT

FOOD stems, leaves, buds and berries in summer; bark and needles in winter; like to lick salt.

SHELTER den alone in rocks or treetops in summer; den together in caves, hollow trees, under downed logs or in buildings in winter.

WATER mostly from food.

RANGE less than ¼ square mile; daily movements up to 400 square feet.

BIG RODENT

Porcupines are the second biggest rodent in Colorado next to the beaver. They weigh up to 30 pounds.

SENSES

Porcupines have very poor eye sight, but an excellent sense of smell for detecting predators.

SOFT BELLY

Porcupines do not have quills on their belly. If a predator is able to flip it onto its back, the porcupine can easily be killed.

family field guide

Raccoon

mount courtesy of Cabela's retail store, Kansas City, KS

PREDATORS
horned owl, hawks, coyote, bobcat and mountain lion; adults have no real predators

HUMAN THREATS
car accidents, nuisance killings

MATING SEASON
February-March

BIRTH SEASON
April-May

LITTER SIZE
2-5

BROKEN FAMILIES In winter, raccoons often nest in attics, chimneys, sheds or under decks. When babies are born in spring and they become more active, they are often trapped as pests. Mother coons are usually trapped and killed or trapped and moved at least fifteen miles away.

AGGRESSIVE AND NIMBLE Raccoons' front hands look very much like a human hand except without a thumb. They open gates and get into garbage cans with ease. They can be very aggressive and are often an annoying visitor. Keep garbage, pets and pet foods inside.

LIVING WITH WILDLIFE To prevent raccoons from moving into attics or sheds, fix all holes and other possible entrances. Cap all chimneys in the spring and fence off areas under decks. Use electric fencing to protect garden areas in summer. Contact animal control services to remove raccoons that have moved in and remember that it is illegal to keep a raccoon as a pet without proper permits.

WINTER SURVIVAL Raccoons continue to feed throughout winter so long as food is available. If temperatures get too cold or snow is too deep, they will stay in their dens for a week or more. Once the weather improves, they continue with their outdoor hunts.

family field guide

HABITAT

FOOD small mammals, frogs, bird eggs, berries, acorns, garbage, dead animals; over 100 different food types have been noted!

SHELTER raccoons find shelter in trees, rock shelters and quiet places in buildings (attics, above garages, etc.).

WATER streams and lakes.

RANGE need only 1/2 square mile in urban areas where food is easy to find, 5-10 square miles along stream banks in wilderness setting.

WATER

Raccoons often dip their food in water before eating it. Some say that they wash their food, but really the water softens their food.

NOSE

Raccoons have a good sense of smell and will return to places where they have sniffed out a food supply.

BRAINS

Raccoons are clever. They work together and can use sticks or rocks as tools to get the food they want.

FINGERS

Raccoon fingers are very nimble. They can open doors, pry apart fence posts and lift lids to garbage containers.

family field guide

Red Fox

SUMMER ONLY   WINTER AND SUMMER

WHEN   WINTER

SUMMER/FALL   SPRING/ WINTER

ROLE

United States Fish and Wildlife Service

PREDATORS
coyote, bear, bobcat

HUMAN THREATS
poisoning, small game hunting/trapping

MATING SEASON
January-February

BIRTH SEASON
March-April

LITTER SIZE
4-5

WANDERING Red foxes wander many miles each night looking for food. They like to live near meadows, grasslands and pastures where small rodents are common and there are few downed trees or rocks to get in their wandering way!

ALL IN THE FAMILY Red fox families usually stay together. After kits are born in spring, the male and female work together to feed the kits. By fall, the kits leave the den to live on their own and the male and female separate. They often rejoin again in mid-winter and mate again in spring.

HUNTING BAN Fox hunting was a tradition in the United Kingdom (England, Northern Ireland, Scotland, Wales and the Channel Islands) for over 400 years. Originally, dogs chased foxes out of the fields and farmers would follow on horseback to get the "pests" out of their crops . Eventually fox hunting became a sport for royalty and upper class citizens. Starting in the mid-1900s people began thinking about cruelty to wildlife. Fox hunting was banned in Scotland in 2002 and in England and Wales in 2005.

THEY'RE EVERYWHERE Red foxes have the largest range of any wild carnivore in the world. They are native to North America, Europe, Asia and northern Africa. They were introduced to Australia in the 1800s.

family field guide

HABITAT

FOOD deer mice, pocket gophers, birds, eggs, cottontails, insects, snakes, frogs, berries, grasses, nuts, dead animals.

SHELTER use underground dens or rock shelters throughout the year; thick winter coat protects them from cold.

WATER streams, lakes, blood from prey.

RANGE 1-25 square miles depending on food.

SMALLEST IN THE FAMILY

Red foxes are the smallest member of the dog family which includes wolves, coyotes and several other fox species.

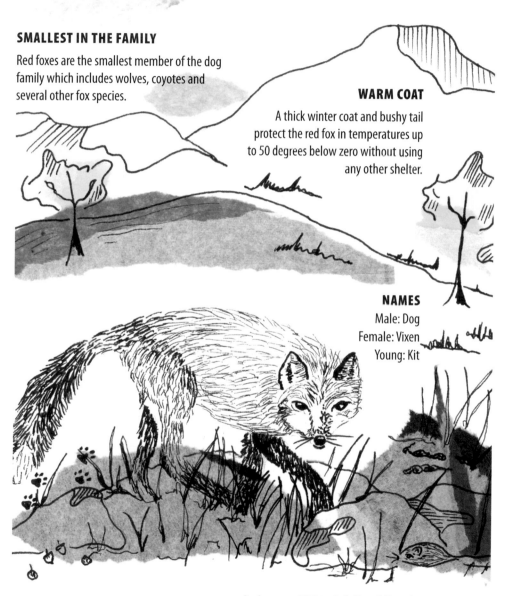

WARM COAT

A thick winter coat and bushy tail protect the red fox in temperatures up to 50 degrees below zero without using any other shelter.

NAMES

Male: Dog
Female: Vixen
Young: Kit

family field guide

Skunk
(Striped Skunk)

WHERE

WHEN   **WINTER**   **FOOD**

ROLE

photo by Robin Henry

PREDATORS
great horned owls

HUMAN THREATS
nuisance killings, car accidents

MATING SEASON
February-March

BIRTH SEASON
May-June

LITTER SIZE
5-8 (avg. 7)

COMING CLEAN Skunk spray is a yellowish, oily liquid and can linger up to 2 weeks. Soap does not wash it off and deodorants are not strong enough to hide the smell. Soaking in tomato soup is a traditional method of cleaning but commercial products are also available to get rid of it.

THE NOSE KNOWS Skunk spray contains molecules called thiols along with molecules of sulfur. Our nose is very sensitive to these molecules such that we avoid the smell. A lot of foods produce sulfur and thiols when they spoil. Natural gas does not contain any odor on its own, but gas companies add thiols and sulfur to the gas so that we can smell when it is leaking!

PROTECTION Even though skunks are fat, slow-moving mammals, their scent protects them from predators. They can spray a mist up to 15 feet that can sting an attacker's eyes. Their stinky protection is so successful that most predators are unsuccessful in their attacks. A skunk's most common threat, however, is the great horned owl which does not have a sense of smell.

STINKY NEIGHBORS Humans are the biggest threat to skunks. Skunks that live under decks or dig burrows beneath houses are pests to dogs and people too. Their stink can be so annoying that people trap and kill skunks near their houses. Most of these house problems take place in winter or early spring when animals are denning near or under a house. Call Animal Control officials to take care of your skunk problem before trying to solve it on your own!

family field guide

HABITAT

FOOD crickets, beetles, grasshoppers, earthworms, snails, birds, eggs, small mammals, dead animals, berries, vegetation.

WATER streams, lakes and vegetation.

SHELTER above ground in thick brush during summer; community dens in underground burrows or below buildings in winter.

RANGE 1-15 square miles depending on food.

WINTER WARMTH

Skunks den together in caves or below houses in winter. They eat weekly, but mostly stay inside their den, quietly warming together.

EYES

Skunks have excellent night vision so they can hunt in the dark.

STRIPES

The stripes are a warning to predators. Like beetles, caterpillars, frogs and other animals, their markings warn off attackers before they strike.

family field guide

Snowshoe Hare

WHERE

WHEN

WINTER

FOOD

ROLE

National Park Service

PREDATORS
fox, coyote, lynx, weasel, marten, bobcat, hawk, owl

HUMAN THREATS
small game hunting

MATING SEASON
April-September

BIRTH SEASON
May-October

LITTER SIZE
2-3 litters, 4-5 young in each litter

FOOD CHAIN Snowshoe hares are an important prey animal in subalpine forests where ground squirrels and other small rodents are less common. Even with litters of 12 newborns every year, snowshoe hares do not overpopulate because so many predators feed on them.

ESCAPE Snowshoe hares are well adapted for escape. If they hear danger, they thump the ground with their big feet to warn others in the area. Next, they sit very still using camouflage to hide. If chased, they are very fast runners, zig-zagging through the forest, never running in a straight line. Even with these escape plans, snowshoe hares are lucky to live one year.

LINKS TO THE LYNX While many animals hibernate, migrate, take to the trees or slow down during the subalpine winter, snowshoe hare and lynx are as active in winter as in summer. Both animals have huge hind feet for getting through snow. Snowshoe hare is the preferred food of the lynx: almost 75% of lynx diet is snowshoe hare! Lynx may travel 60-80 miles to find a snowshoe hare population and many will die in search of food when snowshoe hare populations are low. When snowshoe hare numbers are high, however, lynx populations increase.

CAMOUFLAGE A brown coat in summer and white coat in winter helps with camouflage and winter warmth. White hairs are filled with air instead of coloring which makes it warmer than a colored coat.

family field guide

HABITAT

FOOD *graze* on grasses, buds and leaves in summer; *browse* on evergreen needles and bark in winter.

SHELTER nest above ground in natural depressions next to logs or under brush.

WATER streams, snow, vegetation.

RANGE up to 20 football fields.

PROTECTION

Hares use the forest as shelter from danger and rarely go more than 50 yards away from the forest into meadows or pastures.

FEET

Huge hind feet allow them to run on soft snow without sinking and are used to kick predators during escape.

family field guide

Weasel
(Long-Tailed Weasel)

WHERE

WHEN **WINTER**

FOOD **ROLE**

mount courtesy of ACES

winter coat

LONG OR SHORT? If you see what looks like a baby long-tailed weasel in fall or winter, it is most likely a short-tailed weasel or ermine. Long-tailed and short-tailed weasels are very similar in appearance and behavior, but long-tailed weasels are twice as large.

CHANGING COATS In summer, weasels have a brown body, tan belly and chin and a black-tipped tail. In winter, they are white everywhere except for their black-tipped tail, nose and eyes.

SUPER STRENGTH A weasel can easily kill a pocket gopher, which weighs almost as much as a weasel, and carry it in its mouth, bounding through 8 inches of snow to its own den. Imagine a 60-pound child carrying a 50-pound bag of top soil in its mouth while jumping through 4 feet of snow for a mile! Wow!!!

HUNTERS Like all members of the weasel family, long-tailed weasels are fierce hunters. They walk through burrows of underground rodents, listen for sounds of digging rodents and chase down their prey. Weasels eat 40% of their body weight every day (a 60-pound child eating 96 Quarter Pounders™ every day!).

PREDATORS
coyotes, foxes and owls

HUMAN THREATS
none

MATING SEASON
July-August

BIRTH SEASON
April-May

LITTER SIZE
4-9 (avg. 7)

family field guide

HABITAT

FOOD mice, pocket gophers, voles, pika, chipmunks, ground squirrels, ground-nesting birds.

WATER blood from their prey.

SHELTER underground nests in abandoned burrows, beneath rocks, roots and logs; are lined with grasses and the fur from their prey.

RANGE $1/4$–$1/2$ square mile.

DEADLY COIL

When hunting above ground, a weasel will wrap its long body around its prey to catch it before biting its neck.

TRACKS

When weasels bound, their front feet land together, then the hind feet land together. Their tracks land in a straight line and often make "barbell" markings when their legs drag in deep snow.

LONG AND SKINNY

Their long skinny body is perfect for entering underground burrows and dens.

family field guide

Wyoming Ground Squirrel

WHERE (pastures and meadows)

WHEN   WINTER

ROLE

FOOD

PREDATORS
hawks, dogs, coyote, fox, weasel, badger

HUMAN THREATS
cars, nuisance killings (traps, shooting, poison)

MATING SEASON
April-May

BIRTH SEASON
May-June

LITTER SIZE
3-11 (avg. 5)

photo by Robin Henry

ENTERTAINING As you approach a Wyoming ground squirrel colony, listen for the high-pitched warning call and watch for tails flittering in fast moving circles as they scurry towards the den. Stand still for ten minutes and they may forget about you so you can watch them go about their normal living.

NUISANCE These ground squirrles are often seen as a nuisance because they dig up smooth pastures and because their populations grow fast. Their burrows are just large enough for a cow or horse to twist their ankle when running through a pasture, and the dirt mounds they create destroy smooth golf fairways and school playgrounds. If two pairs of ground squirrels survive the winter in a den on your school playground, and each of them has 10 babies, over twenty animals will be running around your school campus before school lets out in early June.

GROUND SQUIRREL OR PRAIRIE DOG? Wyoming ground squirrels and black-tailed prairie dogs live in similar ecosystems and are easily mistaken for each other. Look for three main differences: Wyoming ground squirrels are smaller, have longer tails, and are a consistent brown color without any white or dark markings on their face.

NAME CHANGE The Wyoming ground squirrel was once called the Richardson's ground squirrel.

family field guide

HABITAT

FOOD grass, flowering plants, shrubs, insects, eggs from ground nesting birds, their own dead on road-sides.

SHELTER underground dens are 15-20 feet long, 4-5 feet below the ground.

WATER mostly from vegetation.

RANGE ½ football field.

FLICKERING TAIL

Watch carefully when Wyoming ground squirrels give their warning call. Not only do they make noise with their voices, they also flick their tail back and forth as another way to get the rest of the colony's attention.

STAND TALL

These ground squirrels stand on their hind feet so that they can look over the tall grasses to see danger.

SLEEPERS

True hibernators, Wyoming ground squirrels hibernate half the year without waking. Even during their active months they sleep away 40% of each day.

family field guide

Appendix

What Do They Eat?

HERBIVORES

Bighorn sheep
Beaver
Chipmunk
Cottontail
Deer mouse
Elk
Marmot
Moose
Mountain goat
Mule deer
Muskrat
Pika
Pocket gopher
Porcupine
Snowshoe hare
Golden-mantled ground squirrel
Wyoming ground squirrel

OMNIVORES

Black bear
Raccoon
Skunk
Red fox (summer/fall)

CARNIVORE

Badger
Bobcat
Coyote
Lynx
Mink
Mountain lion
Pine marten
Red fox (spring/winter)
Long-tailed weasel

TYPES OF FOOD

All herbivores can be food for carnivores except healthy adult moose and elk which are too big to be common prey to any Colorado carnivore. Carnivores are not commonly eaten because they can injure and kill an attacker. Herbivore foods are listed below:

Leaves	Grasses	Berries:
Flowers	Mushrooms	Service berries
Roots	Insect eggs	Juniper berries
Nuts/Seeds	Birds	Raspberries
Tree bark (cambium)	Bird eggs	Thimbleberries
Evergreen needles	Stems	Chokecherries

family field guide

FOOD CHAINS

All animals, including humans, eat food to get energy. If we do not eat food, we do not have the energy to move, to keep ourselves warm, to think properly or to get more food. Energy begins with the sun, then plants absorb energy from the sun, then plant eaters get some of that energy, then meat eaters get some of that energy. Simple food chains look like this:

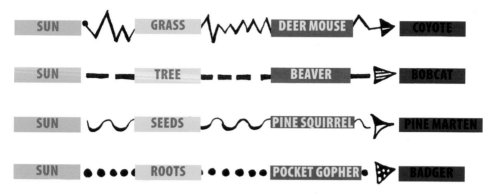

FOOD WEB

The movement of energy through plants and animals is not as simple as a single food chain. A web of arrows finally shows who eats what and who is eaten by whom within an ecosystem. Follow the arrows to see who eats what, and who is eaten by whom in this web. Add your own arrows to complete the web.

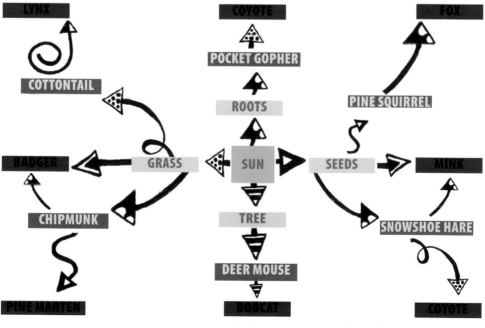

Where Do They Live?

ALPINE SUMMER

Pika
Chipmunk
Marmot
Pocket gopher
Deer mouse
Coyote
Red fox
Elk
Pine marten

Badger
Skunk
Mountain lion
Lynx
Long-tailed weasel
Mule deer
Bighorn sheep
Mountain goat
Golden-mantled ground squirrel

ALPINE WINTER

Pika
Pocket gopher
Deer mouse
Long-tailed weasel
Lynx
Mountain goat
Pine marten

SUBALPINE SUMMER

Chipmunk
Marmot
Bobcat
Elk
Pine squirrel
Deer mouse
Porcupine
Coyote
Red fox
Black bear
Pine marten

Long-tailed weasel
Pocket gopher
Skunk
Mountain lion
Lynx
Golden-mantled ground squirrel
Mule deer
Snowshoe hare
Bighorn sheep
Mountain goat

SUBALPINE WINTER

Snowshoe hare
Pine squirrel
Pocket gopher
Deer mouse
Pine marten
Long-tailed weasel
Lynx
Mountain goat

MONTANE SUMMER

Cottontail
Chipmunk
Marmot
Elk
Pine squirrel
Pocket gopher
Deer mouse
Porcupine
Coyote
Red fox
Pine marten

Black bear
Long-tailed weasel
Badger
Skunk
Mountain lion
Bobcat
Golden-mantled ground squirrel
Mule deer
Bighorn sheep
Wyoming ground squirrel

MONTANE WINTER

Cottontail
Pine squirrel
Pocket gopher
Deer mouse
Coyote
Red fox
Long-tailed weasel
Bighorn sheep
Pine marten

LOWLAND SHRUB/FOREST SUMMER

Cottontail
Chipmunk
Skunk
Bobcat
Pocket gopher
Deer mouse
Porcupine

Coyote
Red fox
Black bear
Long-tailed weasel
Badger
Wyoming ground squirrel
Golden-mantled Ground Squirrel

LOWLAND SHRUB/FOREST WINTER

Cottontail
Pocket gopher
Deer mouse
Mule deer
Bighorn sheep
Long-tailed weasel

Mountain lion
Bobcat
Elk
Coyote
Red fox

family field guide

CLIFFS
Mountain goat
Bighorn sheep

TREE TOPS
Pine squirrel
Pine marten
Porcupine

HOLLOW LOGS
Bobcat	Cottontail
Skunk	Snowshoe hare
Raccoon	Deer mouse
Pine marten	

ROCK DENS
Marmot
Pika

WATER
Muskrat
Beaver
Mink

BURROWS
Cottontail	Long-tailed weasel
Chipmunk	Pocket gopher
Red fox	Coyote (nursing)
Badger	Mountain lion (nursing)

Golden-mantled ground squirrel
Wyoming ground squirrel

NO SHELTER
Elk	Mountain lion
Mule deer	Mountain goat
Bighorn sheep	Black bear (summer)
Moose	Coyote

THICK BRUSH
Cottontail	Deer mouse
Snowshoe hare	Porcupine
Bobcat	

When Are They Active?

These categories are guidelines about when a species is most active, but animals do not always follow these rules. For example, most humans are diurnal, but some people work at night and have to sleep during the day to get some rest. Individual animals may behave differently from this list. Also, animals may behave differently throughout seasons, food shortages, hunger, following territorial fights or during dispersal.

NOCTURNAL

Badger*
Bobcat
Coyote*
Deer mouse
Lynx
Mountain lion*
Pine marten*
Pocket gopher*
Porcupine
Raccoon
Red fox*
Snowshoe hare
Skunk

DIURNAL

Badger*
Bighorn sheep
Black bear*
Chipmunk
Coyote*
Marmot
Mink
Moose
Mountain goat
Mountain lion*
Mule deer (winter)
Pika
Pine squirrel
Pine marten*
Pocket gopher*
Long-tailed weasel
Golden-manteled ground squirrel
Wyoming ground squirrel

CREPUSCULAR

Beaver
Black bear*
Cottontail
Elk
Mule deer (summer)
Muskrat
Red fox*

*animal commonly fits into two different behavior patterns

family field guide

Winter Survival

Winter creates three challenges to animals: temperatures are cold, snow is difficult to walk through and food is difficult to find. Animals use different strategies to survive the cold temperatures, deep snow and shortage of food.

SNOW LOVERS

Mountain goat
Snowshoe hare
Lynx
Pine squirrel
Pine marten
Moose
Mink
Cottontail
Deer mouse
Pocket gopher
Long-tailed weasel
Pika

SNOW TOLERATORS

Badger
Beaver
Raccoon
Skunk
Porcupine
Muskrat

HOW DO SNOW LOVERS SURVIVE?

BIG FEET (lynx and snowshoe hare)
LIVE IN TREES (pine squirrel and marten)
LIVE UNDER SNOW (deer mouse)
LIVE UNDERGROUND (pocket gopher)
WARM WINTER COAT (fox and mountain goat)
LONG LEGS (moose)

MIGRATORS

Elk
Mule deer
Bighorn sheep
Mountain lion
Coyote
Red fox
Bobcat

HIBERNATORS

Black bear
Marmot
Chipmunk
Wyoming ground squirrel
Golden-mantled ground squirrel

How Big Are They?

Animals are arranged in order from smallest to largest based on average weight. Measurements are based mostly on information from *Mammals Of Colorado* by Fitzgerald, Meaney and Armstrong.

ANIMAL	WEIGHT	LENGTH
Deer mouse	¼-1 ounce	5-7 inches
Least chipmunk	½-1 ounce	7-9 inches
Pocket gopher	3-8 ounces	6-9 inches
Pika	4-8 ounces	6-9 inches
Long-tailed weasel	4-12 ounces	13-17 inches
Pine squirrel	6-9 ounces	12-14 inches
Golden-mantled ground squirrel	6-10 ounces	10-12 inches
Wyoming ground squirrel	11-17 ounces	10-13 inches
Mink	1-2 pounds	19-28 inches
Pine marten	1-3 pounds	18-30 inches
Muskrat	1-4 pounds	17-22 inches
Cottontail	2-2.5 pounds	13-16 inches
Snowshoe hare	2-3 pounds	14-21 inches
Marmot	4-11 pounds	19-27 inches
Skunk	3-10 pounds	23-30 inches
Red fox	7-15 pounds	37-41 inches
Raccoon	7-25 pounds	24-37 inches
Porcupine	9-40 pounds	25-37 inches
Bobcat	11-30 pounds	29-39 inches
Lynx	11-33 pounds	26-42 inches
Badger	13-31 pounds	26-35 inches
Coyote	18-45 pounds	41-55 inches
Beaver	35-70 pounds	33-47 inches
Mule deer	85-175 pounds	49-77 inches
Mountain lion	80-200 pounds	59-105 inches
Bighorn sheep	110-275 pounds	49-77 inches
Mountain goat	88-300 pounds	37-67 inches
Black bear	200-500 pounds	55-78 inches
Elk	500-900 pounds	82-110 inches
Moose	up to 1300 pounds	94-11 inches

family field guide

How Much Space?

Animals are arranged in order from smallest home range to largest based on the largest possible area a species may use. Home ranges vary greatly depending on amount of food within a given area, but this chart gives a general idea of how much space a species may use. Numbers are based mostly on information from *Mammals Of Colorado* by Fitzgerald, Meaney and Armstrong.

ANIMAL	HOME RANGE
Deer mouse	$1/2$ football field
Pocket gopher	$1/2$ football field
Pika	$1/2$ football field
Muskrat	$1/2$ football field
Wyoming ground squirrel	$1/2$ football field
Pine squirrel	1-2 football fields
Least chipmunk	2-3 football fields
Marmot	2-4 football fields
Beaver	3-7 football fields
Cottontail	1-10 football fields
Snowshoe hare	2-20 football fields
Golden-mantled ground squirrel	2-30 football fields
Porcupine	$1/4$ square mile
Long-tailed weasel	$1/4$-$1/2$ square mile
Badger	$1/2$-1 square mile
Mink	1-3 square miles
Pine marten	1-6 square miles
Raccoon	5-10 square miles
Skunk	1-15 square miles
Mountain goat	7-15 square miles
Bobcat	9-20 square miles
Red fox	1-25 square miles
Coyote	10-50 square miles
Black bear	5-75 square miles
Lynx	10-95 square miles
Mountain lion	15-320 square miles
*Moose	2-4 square mile ranges (5-40 mile migration)
*Bighorn sheep	3-10 square mile ranges (3-10 mile migration)
*Mule deer	5-10 square mile ranges (5-10 mile migration)
*Elk	3-20 square mile ranges (5-35 mile migration)

*animal migrates each fall and spring. Its summer and winter range may be smaller than animals listed above it, but migrating animals are grouped together in order of smallest to largest seasonal range.

family field guide

Relatives

Animals are arranged with their relatives based on their scientific classification.

KINGDOM Animalia
PHYLUM Chordata
CLASS Mammalia

ORDER Rodent

Least chipmunk
Marmot
Wyoming ground squirrel
Golden-mantled ground squirrel
Pine squirrel
Pocket gopher
Beaver
Deer mouse
Muskrat
Porcupine

ORDER Lagamorph

Pika
Cottontail
Snowshoe hare

ORDER Carnivora

FAMILY Dog (canine)

Coyote
Red fox

FAMILY Cat (feline)

Bobcat
Mountain lion
Lynx

FAMILY Weasel (mustelidae)

Pine marten
Long-tailed weasel
Short-tailed weasel
Mink
Badger
Striped skunk

ORDER Artiodactyla

FAMILY Bovid (bovidae)

Mountain goat
Bighorn sheep

FAMILY Deer (cervidae)

Elk
Mule deer
Moose

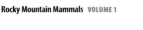

family field guide

Awards

Following is a list of animals that have exceptional characteristics among Colorado's Mammals.

LARGEST MAMMAL

Moose

LARGEST CARNIVORE

Black bear

LARGEST RODENT
(IN NORTH AMERICA)

Beaver

BEST DEFENSES

Skunk

Porcupine

MOST ABUNDANT

Deer mouse

MOST WIDESPREAD MAMMAL
(IN NORTH AMERICA)

Mountain lion

BEST CAMOUFLAGE

Snowshoe hare

Long-tailed Weasel

WARMEST WINTER COAT

Mountain goat

Red fox

WORST HUMAN CONFLICTS

Black bear

Beaver

Skunk

Raccoon

MOST SECRETIVE

Mountain lion

Bobcat

Lynx

family field guide

Glossary

Adaptablility An animal's ability to change its behavior or body so that it can survive.

Alpine tundra The life zone above timberline (11,400-14,433 feet in Colorado). It is the coldest and windiest ecosystem with only 3 months growing season each year.

Altricial Babies born unable to see, without fur and helpless for the first part of their life. Precocial is the opposite of atricial.

Antler Bone that grows out of the skull of an animal. It falls off each year, then regrows again.

Birth season The months when babies are born.

Browse To eat shrubs.

Buck Male deer.

Bugle The name used to describe the sound made by a male elk during mating season.

Bull Male elk.

Camouflage An animal's ability to blend into its surroundings. For example, some animals' coats are the same color as the forest, rocks, snow or shadows where they live.

Carnivore An animal that eats mostly meat.

Carrion A dead and decomposing animal.

Community Plants and animals living together in the same environment.

Cornice A snowdrift hanging over a ridge caused by wind blowing from the windward to the leeward side.

Cow Female elk.

Crepuscular Actively eating and moving at dawn and dusk and resting in mid-day and mid-night.

Deforestation Cutting of trees in a way that destroys animal habitat.

Delayed implantation After a female becomes pregnant, the egg waits for days or months before it starts growing so that the baby will be born during the right conditions.

Development Building houses and roads in a way that destroys animal habitat.

Dispersal The time when babies leave their mother to live on their own.

Diurnal Most actively eating and moving during mid-day and resting at night. May be active at dawn and dusk.

Doe Female deer.

Ecosystem The interactions between plants, animals and non-living things within a specific environment.

Ecotone Where two different ecosystems meet. In many cases, animals prefer ecotones because they can find different needs very close together. For example, they can have good visibility in a meadow near the protection of a forest.

Ermine Another name for the short-tailed weasel.

Esker A mound of soil shaped like a snake created by a pocket gopher tunneling through winter snow, filling the snow tunnel with soil. When the snow melts, the soil rests obviously on the spring and summer ground.

Gestation period The amount of time a baby has to grow from when the female becomes pregnant to when the baby is born.

Graze To eat grass.

Gray wolf A type of wolf that was native to Colorado, but is now extinct in Colorado.

Grizzly bear A type of bear that was native to Colorado, but is now extinct in Colorado.

Hare A small mammal identified by its long ears and hopping behavior, hares are born with fur and are able to see at birth. They live alone in nests built above ground.

Harem A group of female animals that the male mates with during mating season; most commonly associated with deer and elk.

Herbivore An animal that eats mostly plants.

Hibernate To be inactive. The heart and breathing rates slow and the body temperature cools so the body is able to stay alive until the animal is ready to become active again.

Hindquarters The rump and back legs of an animal.

Horn A growth of keratin (the same material that makes our fingernails) that grows out of the skull. Horns never fall off.

Human threats Interactions that take place between people and animals that can cause harm to an animal or to its entire species.

Introduced Plants and animals that did not live in an area originally, but were placed there by humans whether on purpose or by accident.

Krummholz Stunted trees near timberline.

Lagomorph The order of animals that includes hares, pikas and rabbits.

Leeward side The side of the mountain that is protected from the wind.

Lichens A fungus growing together with an algae that forms a crust-like growth on rocks and trees. The fungus gets nutrients from the rock or tree on which it grows while the algae photosynthesizes to get energy from the sun.

Life zone A place where a certain community lives. In the Rocky Mountains, life zones are determined by elevation except for the riparian zone which can extend through any elevation.

Litter size The number of young born at one time.

Lodge The name given to a beaver house.

Lowland shrub and forest The life zone between 5,000-8,000 feet which includes sage communities, shrubland communities and pinyon-juniper forest communities.

Mating season The months when a female animal is able to become pregnant.

Midden pile The pile of leftover pine cone scales dropped at the base of evergreen trees by pine squirrels as they take seeds out of the cones.

Montane forest A forest life zone between 5,600-9,000 feet which supports aspen groves, douglas fir, lodgepole pine and ponderosa pine communities.

Native A plant or animal that has originally lived in an area without human introduction.

Nictitating membrane A clear, third eyelid used to protect the eye while still allowing the animal to see.

Nocturnal Actively feeding and moving at night while resting during mid-day. The animal may be active at dawn and dusk.

Nuisance killing Killing of animals because they interrupt human activity. Examples include the killing of bears when they feed in houses or campsites. Animals commonly killed include: skunks, beavers, muskrats, coyote, bobcat, mountain lion, wyoming ground squirrel and porcupine.

Omnivore An animal that eats plants and meat equally or almost equally.

Points The number of spikes that branch off of deer, elk and moose antlers; also called tines.

Precocial Babies born able to see, fully furred and able to move around on their own. The opposite of precocial is atricial.

Predator An animal that hunts other animals.

Prey An animal that is hunted by other animals.

Problem bear The name used to describe a bear that commonly finds food in houses and campgrounds.

Pronking The style of running used by a deer when it leaps through the air, landing on all four legs at the same time. This combined style of running and jumping allows them to move quickly through shrubs by jumping over them. Also called stotting.

Rabbits A small mammal identified by its long ears and hopping behavior, rabbits are born blind and without fir. They live in community burrows below ground. Cottontails are examples of a Colorado rabbit.

Reintroduction Occurs when an animal lived in an area, became extinct, then members of species are captured and placed in the area where they once lived. Moose and Lynx are examples of Colorado mammals that have been reintroduced.

Riparian The ecosystem that occurs along the edges of lakes, streams and creeks and within wetlands.

Rut A name used to describe a male elk's mating season. The males are in their rut.

Scree field A large area covered entirely with rocks the size of dinner plates or smaller.

Semi-aquatic An animal that is equally coordinated on land and in water.

Shed A word used to describe deer, elk or moose dropping their antlers. (Examples: He found a deer shed; The deer shed its antlers in March.

Stotting The style of running used by a deer when it leaps through the air, landing on all four legs at the same time. This combined style of running and jumping allows them to move quickly through shrubs by jumping over them. Also called pronking.

Subalpine forest A forested life zone at 9,000-11,400 feet that supports the Engelmann Spruce and Subalpine Fir community.

Subnivean Under the snow.

Talus slope A large area covered entirely with rocks larger than a dinner plate.

Timberline The altitude above sea level where trees stop growing (around 11,400 feet in Colorado).

Tines The number of spikes that branch off of deer, elk and moose antlers; also called points.

Torpor A resting state in which an animal's heart and breathing rates slow, and their body temperature drops slightly. Used to survive winter in the mountains.

Transients Animals that have no permanent home, but rather roam a great distance, usually in search of food.

Velvet The soft tissue that covers antlers as they grow. Velvet is filled with blood vessels and nutrients that allow the bone to grow and become an antler. Velvet sheds in late summer when the antlers have stopped growing.

Vole A small rodent, similar in size to a deer mouse.

Windward side The side of a mountain or structure that faces towards the wind; features of the mountain or structure are often affected by the wind.

Index

family field guide

family field guide

References

Burt, Willliam H., Grossenheider, Richard P. 1980. *Peterson Field Guide to the Mammals: North America North of Mexico*. Houghton Mifflin Company.

Fitzgerald, J.; Meaney C.; and Armstrong, D. 1994. *Mammals of Colorado*. Denver Museum of Natural History and University Press of Colorado.

Huggins, Janis Lindsey. 2004. *Wild At Heart: A Natural History Guide Dedicated to Snowmass, Aspen and the Maroon Bells Wilderness*. The Town of Snowmass Village.

Young, Mary Taylor. 2000. *On The Trail of Colorado Critters*. Denver Museum of Natural History.

Whitaker, John O., Elman, Robert. 1980. *The Audubon Society Field Guide to North American Mammals*. Knopf.

Halfpenny, James C. 2001. *Scats and Tracks of the Rocky Mountains: A Field Guide to the Signs of 70 Wildlife Species*. Globe Pequot Press.

family field guide